THE FINAL WHISTLE

Life and Times of K D Singh 'Babu'

THE FINAL WHISTLE

Life and Times of K D Singh 'Babu'

Kunwar Raghavendra Singh

B L O O M S B U R Y
NEW DELHI • LONDON • OXFORD • NEW YORK • SYDNEY

BLOOMSBURY INDIA
Bloomsbury Publishing India Pvt. Ltd
Second Floor, LSC Building No. 4, DDA Complex, Pocket C – 6 & 7,
Vasant Kunj, New Delhi 110070

BLOOMSBURY, BLOOMSBURY PRIME and the Diana logo are
trademarks of Bloomsbury Publishing Plc

First published in 2018

ISBN: 978-93-88038-00-3

2 4 6 8 10 9 7 5 3 1

Typeset by Prepsol Enterprises Pvt Ltd
Printed and bound in India by EIH Limited

Contents

Foreword

For me, K D SINGH 'BABU' remains the most charismatic and distinguished sports personality that I have ever come across in my life and I feel greatly honoured to write the foreword for this book. Though I was very briefly associated with him as one of his trainees this book has now enabled me to know more about him. The vivid description of his artistic game as narrated by sports critics of his time is mind boggling. Reading through the book one may now understand why he was honoured by Helms Athletic Foundation, Los Angeles for being the best athlete of Asia and best hockey player of the world at the 1952 Helsinki Olympic Games. To have been honoured by a world sports body for individual performance and contribution in a sport like hockey speaks volumes about his magical game. It is absolutely true that if India dominated at the 1948 and 1952 hockey Olympic Games it was largely because of K D Singh 'Babu'.

It was in 1970 that I first came in touch with K D Singh 'Babu' during the All India Invitation Hockey Tournament in Lucknow. Initially there was some trouble in my selection and I was asked to leave the camp but it was K D Singh 'Babu' who called me back and I got the great break in my playing career. At the 1972 Much Olympics I had been playing as a left-out.

K D Singh 'Babu' had a very keen eye and no one could understand the strong and weak points of a player better than him. He had a sixth sense. At the 1972 Munich Olympics I had been playing as a left-out but somehow K D Singh 'Babu' felt that I could do much better as a centre-forward. In the match against Holland he shifted me to centre-forward position after Holland had scored first. Immediately thereafter I scored the equalizer and later on Mukhbain Singh scored the decider and we clinched the bronze for India. He was a master strategist and the first one who took up teaching hockey on board.

Apart from being a great hockey player and a coach par excellence, K D Singh 'Babu' was a great human being. Many a sportsmen and women owe their lively hood to him. He was also the coach of Indian Airlines team and it was on his recommendations that the players got a job in the Airlines.

K D Singh 'Babu' was one of those rare sportsmen who could take up any sport with comparative ease. He was also an excellent marksman. While we were preparing for 1972 Munich Olympics at Lucknow he would often take the entire team out for a partridge and quail shoot in his home District of Barabanki. We had to carry our sticks to beat the bushes and at the end of a tiring day he would smile and say, 'Well boys this is a part of your training'. Never did we see him miss any fast flying bird.

I have played under so many good Indian coaches during my career from 1970 to 1978 for India and thereafter for Indian Airlines. I will rate Mr. K D Singh 'Babu' the best coach that I ever played under.

This book also covers his life away from hockey which makes very interesting reading. Sine this is the first time that his complete life story has been put between the two covers I am sure readers would wonder if there has been any other sports personality like him. He was the rarest among the rare in the world of sports.

B P Govinda

Acknowledgements

K.D. Singh 'Babu' passed away on 27 March 1978, and yet ever since, I never even imagined that one day, I would be writing his biography.

All these years, while all of us in the family always used to talk about him and still do, it was felt that apart from us and some others who knew him intimately, his achievements remained largely hidden from the public eye.

Then it happened all of a sudden. It was my sister, Bindu, who inspired me to take up this task. In the beginning, I was a bit hesitant about whether I would ever be able to make any headway, but she prevailed on me, and today it is purely her perseverance that has enabled me to achieve what I initially thought was a near impossible job.

I also wish to thank my wife, Nimmi, who always got me re-started whenever I disengaged owing to other pressing matters.

I started working on this biography in the year 2012 and it has taken quite a long time to complete. To put together the life of K.D. Singh Babu on and off the field, right from his early days, as a running story has not been an easy job. There were many unforced interruptions and every time I resumed writing, I had to revert to what I had written until then and cross-check to see that the chain of events were well-linked. It is now the third draft that I find is in perfect order.

As I proceeded to make the first draft, I engaged with a lot of people. By the year 2012, the only one alive and present from the previous generation was my father, Dr Kr Suresh Singh, and I had many sessions with him while penning this biography.

Though, unfortunately, he is not with us anymore, I fail for words to express my gratitude to him and at the same time I regret that the script could not be completed during his lifetime.

I also wish to thank my two elder cousins, Kr Vishwanath Singh and Kr Mahendra Singh for many valuable anecdotes connected with the life and game of K.D. Singh Babu. Kr Mahendra Singh was also a very good hockey player and he represented the All India University Hockey Eleven as a right-in. He had been very closely associated with K.D. Singh Babu when he was still active in the 1950s and as such, had been a witness to many glorious 'magic shows'.

The major source of information drawn on for this book has been a collection of newspaper clippings that were carefully pasted in an album by K.D. Singh Babu himself. I am greatly indebted to his sons, Kr Dhirendra Singh and Kr.Vishwavijay Singh, for having allowed me to use this rare collection of newspaper reportage as also the memorable photographs that have been reproduced in this biography. I have also drawn extensively from articles published in *K.D. Singh Memorial Society* magazines published in 1981 and 1982 which were edited by Shri S.N. Kapoor who was also a sports critic of that time. Almost all the articles are by those who mattered in the field of hockey, such as R.S. Gentle who played as a full-back with him in the 1952 Olympics, former Olympic Captain Charanjit Singh, Dr A.C. Chaterjee who was an official of the Indian Hockey Federation, as well as his two elder brothers, namely Kr Shukdeo Singh 'Mohan' and Kr Naresh Singh 'Raja', both of who were leading hockey players of their time and sadly missed the chance to play alongside him in the Olympics had they been held in 1944.

My heart goes out to my daughter, Radhika, who never stopped asking from across the sea about how the book was shaping up. Though now settled in the US, not a day passed when she would not want to know about the progress of the biography with very encouraging words, 'Oh Dad, I know you can do it.' Thanks Radhika, for the confidence that you had in me.

I also wish to thank my friend, Chander Prakash, of Universal Book Sellers here at Lucknow, who helped in many ways that only I know.

Lastly, I would like to thank two former Olympians, Shri B.P. Govinda and Janab Aslam Sher Khan. As I was contemplating taking up this task, I had telephonic conversations with both of them. Their enthusiasm knew no bounds and I really felt motivated. Both of them conveyed to me that if I could really put forth his story between two covers, it would be a fitting tribute to a great hockey player.

Hence, with the blessings of many, I burned the midnight oil in an attempt to rekindle memories of a 'SuperStar' who was born to be remembered for centuries to come.

Special thanks to Shri B.P. Govinda, former Olympian, for having ceded to my request to write the Foreword for this book.

I am grateful to my friend Ravi Kapoor who has done an excellent job in improving the photographs that have been used in this book.

Kunwar Raghavendra Singh

Preface

To gild refined gold, to paint the lily...
Is wasteful and ridiculous excess.

—*Shakespeare*

The sport of hockey as we see it played today has come a long way, having changed drastically from the yesteryear pattern of fine dribbling and body swerves to a game of mostly hit-and-run. Gone are the days of individual run–ups and pattern weaving that were the main attraction of the game. The beauty of field goals has become a rarity. Many believe that this is a fallout of the metamorphosis of the playing surface from grass turf to astro turf. While this may be somewhat true, former New Zealand captain C.V. Walter begged to differ when he commented, 'Dhyan Chand, Roop Singh, Shahbuddin, Sultan Khan and Penninger could do more with a hockey ball on a rugby field than most of the moderns on astro turf.' He further added, 'I think of a forward line consisting of Shahbuddin, K.D. Singh 'Babu', Dhyan Chand, Roop Singh and Jaffar. I think of its operation on an astro turf. I shudder to think of the manner [in which] it would sweep the moderns into the dustbin of history.'

This biography is about a big game hunter who came to be known as the best hockey player of the world who was none else but Padmashree Kunwar Digvijay Singh 'Babu', captain of the gold medal-winning Indian hockey team at the Helsinki Olympic Games, 1952. His name became synonymous with the game of hockey in the annals of Indian sporting history. Popularly known as 'Babu', he was often called 'Hockey Babu' by some in the media as his name grew enmeshed with the game. As I sat down to write his biography, I found it to be a very daunting task and I could not agree more with Shakespeare's words quoted above. K.D. Singh

'Babu' was one of the most illustrious and colourful personalities in the international arena of sports of the time. In my writing, I have tried my best to cover almost everything about his game as I possibly could and I hope that readers will recognise the divine magic this star sportsman possessed not only absolutely thrilling but also unbelieveably unmatched. I have tried to document his personal life based on what I can recollect from memory as also by way of conversations with people who had known him intimately.

WHY THIS BOOK?

For quite some time I had been contemplating writing this biography, as the autobiography penned by K.D. Singh 'Babu' himself got lost, most unfortunately, soon after his demise. It was a great loss. I had seen the manuscript; it contained chapters about the great stalwarts of his time, including Dhyan Chand. More importantly, the script offered a lucid description of every positional aspect of play. It was rather like a textbook on how to play hockey based on his personal thoughts, a guidebook of sorts which would have been the only one of its kind. Now a crucial point to be noted is that this biography comes at a time when there is a furious demand by a certain group that Major Dhyan Chand be honoured with the Bharat Ratna. Though this biography in no way lays a counter claim for K.D. Singh Babu, whatever has been written about his magical game by various leading sports critics of that time shall certainly bring into focus the contentious issue of debate as to who has been the greatest hockey player of all time? And this is exactly why this biography shall generate immense interest among readers far and wide.

Opinions may differ, but one story holds true till the other is told. It is rather unfortunate that though most of the hockey fans and even players of today know about him, yet what all was written about his game never surfaced, except in very close quarters. In this biography I have made an attempt to piece together all the events of his life, right from the time of his first exposure in an exhibition hockey match to his last days, in the form of a running story. I am quite sure readers will find what distinguished him from others as the unstoppable hockey wizard that he truly was.

His artistry was first noticed in the year 1937 when, at the tender age of sixteen, he made his first big bang appearance in a match in Delhi. Major Dhyan Chand, the biggest legend the game had seen until then, had just announced his retirement after the Berlin Olympics held in 1936, and sentiment was rife that a master juggler like him would never take to the field again. Under the dark, menacing clouds of World War II, the Olympics could not be held in the years 1940 and 1944 and the game of hockey was limited to national level matches only. Major Dhyan Chand was still active in the 40s and by no stretch of imagination could hockey fans visualise any other player on the horizon who could possibly replicate his magic or even come anywhere close to his skill. Little did one know that Barabanki, an obscure district of Uttar Pradesh, was about to spring a surprise. Unknown to most, a young man named K.D. Singh, soon to earn the affectionate sobriquet 'Babu', who hailed from this district, was making rapid strides in this direction. This young sportsman would ultimately go on to be acclaimed as the best hockey player of the world. It was no easy job to emerge from the shadow of the great Dhyan Chand, yet K.D. Singh Babu achieved this with great style and confidence. Very soon, he became the cynosure of all eyes and a new standard of the game was set.

By the year 1945, he was already being compared to the great Dhyan Chand. K.D. Singh Babu was only twenty-three years of age then. Playing under the captaincy of the great Dhyan Chand on a tour of East Africa in 1946–47, he totally eclipsed him by scoring 70 goals as against 63 by the wizard. From then on, there was no looking back. A new wizard had arrived on the scene.

As preparations for the 1948 Olympics were in progress, the press painted a very gloomy picture. Most of them opined that now since the Dhyan Chand era had come to an end, India would have a tough time putting up a good show. However, it was for K.D. Singh Babu to prove everyone wrong. Ironically, most of the good English players had emigrated and star Muslim players had opted to move to Pakistan after partition. The impact that all these players made could be gauged from the fact that though Pakistan could make it only to the semi-finals, England stormed into the finals after beating Pakistan. And Holland too had fielded a strong team, so much so that in the semis, they shocked everyone by scoring first against India.

K.D. Singh Babu's strong showing during the 1946–47 tour of East Africa under the captainship of Major Dhyan Chand was still fresh in the memories of hockey fans, particularly the Indian spectators who had gathered in large numbers to see him play and repeat the miracles. And indeed, he disappointed no one. As narrated by Dr A.C. Chaterjee, the team manager, in an article which appeared in *K.D. Singh Memorial Society* magazine: 'Every supporter had pinned hopes on K.D. Singh Babu, and shouts of "Babu, Babu, come on Babu" could be heard all over the arena. It was largely K.D. Singh Babu who had completely mesmerised the dogged England defense in the finals with his brilliant performance.' K.D. Singh Babu cast his magic spell at a time when deep mines were laid in the form of a formidable and packed English defense. He always managed to dribble past a maze of world-class opposition to hand-feed his other forwards.

So far as playmaking and scoring were concerned, he had no parallel. In 1951, he led a team to East Africa. By this time, he had firmly put his stamp of authority on the game and out of a total of 270 goals, he alone scored 93, which is a record by itself.

Despite his great show on this tour, the Indian Hockey Federation (IHF) bosses tried to sideline him for captaincy of the Helsinki Olympic-bound team in 1952. Politics in sport had taken roots. However, though his name was finally announced to lead the team to Helsinki Olympics, doubts were being raised about his capability to keep alive the glory. Writing exclusively for *Times of India*, Rex Rodrigues, who was a team member of the 1948 Olympics, penned a very mordacious column on the prospects of the Indian team and commented that India has only a fifty-fifty chance of retaining the gold. One fails to understand why he came down with such a scathing remark, but it was obvious that since he was a member of the 1948 Olympic team, he had a measure of the strength of other frontline teams which were by then packed with the dual merits of a good defense and strike capability. However, contrary to general belief, he brought the world to its feet with his magical performance. A big game hunter had silenced his critics. India trounced Holland by the biggest margin in the finals.

In 1953, he zoomed past all other players when the Los Angeles-based World Helms Foundation awarded him the coveted World Helms Trophy and declared him the Best Athlete of Asia and Best Hockey Player of the World.

Before the 1956 Melbourne Olympics, a team by the name of Delhi Wanderers was sent to New Zealand to play exhibition matches. The tour was covered in *Sports and Pastime* by C.V. Walter, former New Zealand captain. C.V. Walter had seen both Dhyan Chand and K.D. Singh Babu in action. His description of the wizardry of K.D. Singh Babu is a treat to read; no player in the world of hockey has ever been so highly praised by a person who himself was a great hockey player of his time.

The New Zealand magic upset many in the IHF who collectively desired to sideline K.D. Singh Babu for the next Olympic Games at Melbourne. A smear campaign was launched against him regarding his age and suitability for the top job. Ironically though, he was selected into the team. This would have been his third consecutive Olympic participation but sensing trouble, he refused to attend the training camp and quietly walked out of the team.

The performance of the 1956 Olympics team said it all. India which had reigned supreme in the two preceding Olympics, just managed to retain the gold. The absence of the great 'playmaker' was what made the difference. No forward line player could match him in piercing the opposition defense. As the 1958 Asian Games to be held in Tokyo were fast approaching and sensing that India would be at the receiving end without K.D. Singh Babu in the forward line, AFS (Bobby) Talyarkhan, the most fierce and most feared sport critic of that time, took the IHF to task. Writing for *Bombay Chronicle*, he fired column after column and cautioned the IHF that if they wanted India to win, they had no option but to request K.D. Singh Babu to reconsider his decision and to see that he agreed to play for the country. But the damage had been done and K.D. Singh Babu refused to give it a second thought. India surrendered its supremacy to Pakistan not only at the 1958 Asiads but also at the 1960 Olympics.

Despite having refused to play for India at the past two events due to the high-handedness of some IHF officials, he continued to play in the nationals and made his last appearance in competitive hockey in 1958. Vivid descriptions of his masterly game form the core of this biography.

S.N. Kapoor, former editor of *Swatantra Bharat*, a local daily in Lucknow, who was also a sport critic while editing the first K.D. Singh Babu Memorial Society magazine, 1981, wrote:

'Some commentators and sports critics were inclined to believe that he was a shade better than Dhyan Chand. These assumptions are based on facts... when Dhyan Chand was at the peak of his career, that is [in] 1928, 1932 and 1936, the opposing teams were too weak. At the 1928 Olympics, hockey had just been reintroduced after a long gap. Then again at the 1932 Olympics, only three teams participated, namely India, Japan and USA. Since USA and Japan hardly played any good competitive hockey, it was virtually a walkover for India. At the 1936 Berlin Olympic Games, the opposing teams were no match and apart from known three teams, that is India, Holland and Germany, the rest of the participating nations (Denmark, France, Belgium, Switzerland, Afghanistan, USA, Japan and Hungary) were hardly a force to reckon with. It is also on record that in a practice match against Germany, the Indian side led by Dhyan Chand lost by a margin of 4–1. Here, it is significant to note that Dhyan Chand had the support of players from an undivided India. The Indian squad got so panicky that they had to hurriedly requisition the services of AIS Dara to strengthen the side to avoid an upset.'

In comparison to what has been said above, the entire scenario changed after the partition of India; K.D. Singh Babu had to face a tough opposition and the country was left with little choice as many good players had left. But this had no effect on the Houdini of Indian Hockey. He was a team all by himself and proved his supremacy in a most significant way.

There remains absolutely no doubt that Dhyan Chand was one of the greatest that the hockey world had seen, but the most debatable point when the two stalwarts are compared undoubtedly brings into focus factors that have been elaborated upon earlier. Comparative analysis points to a telling fact, while K.D. Singh Babu faced choppy waters, Dhyan Chand faced weak opposition.

This brings me to a conversation I had with my father on two issues, a few years ago. Age-wise, my father, Kr Suresh Singh, was immediately junior to K.D. Singh and my father was also a hockey player who had captained the Lucknow University team. I put two questions to him. First, I asked him as to who in his opinion was a better hockey player: Dhyan Chand or K.D. Singh Babu. He paused for a while and then said very frankly, 'Very difficult to decide'. The next question that I asked was whether it is true that K.D. Singh created the then India forward Balbir Singh Sr. I based this question on the various comments of sports critic AFS Talyarkhan and fellow hockey player Raghbir Lal Sharma. To this he smilingly replied, 'Had it not been Balbir Singh, he would have created someone else.' Creating players was one of K.D. Singh Babu's greatest merits. He created players who would have otherwise been relegated to oblivion.

While most players sidelined themselves after retirement, K.D. Singh Babu continued to be on the field till his last days. His trainees included school boys and national level players. He played and coached hockey like a chess grandmaster. Paying tribute to him, former Olympian Aslam Sher

Khan said, 'He was the only one who demonstrated in the field what he taught on the board.' Recalling his playing days in an interview given to *Times Sport* in 2011, Saiyad Ali Sibtain Naqvi, a former hockey player now settled in Oman as sports consultant of Oman Hockey Association said, 'My most important moment was that of having played the game with the SuperStar Kunwar Digvijay Singh Babu in [the] 1950s.' He further added, 'K.D. Singh Babu was the best hockey player I have ever come across. He was the greatest playmaker. His dribbling and ball control was amazing. It was as if he had a sixth sense about the game, he could literally predict the moves.'

Speaking at a function of K.D. Singh Babu Memorial sub-junior tournament in Lucknow, former Indian captain and Olympian B.P. Govinda was very categorical in expressing his opinion when he said, 'If any sportsman is to be considered for Bharat Ratna, then the honour must go to K.D. Singh Babu.' In a Facebook comment, former Ranji Trophy player Ashok Bambi wrote: 'K.D. Singh Babu was one of the greatest in the sporting history of the country. He will be remembered for centuries. He was not only a great sportsman, he even lent a helping hand to hundreds of sportsmen and women by getting them jobs.'

He was not only the best hockey player of the world but, more appropriately, he was a rare sports personality. A complete sportsman and a true genius, he could pick up any sporting activity like a duck takes to water. Football, tennis, badminton, cricket and golf came easy to him. Not many know that he was as accomplished in football as he was in hockey.

Apart from field sports, many remember him for his other hobbies. He was a sharpshooter, an excellent marksman with the gun and rifle. Use of firearms came easily to him right from childhood as it was a family recreation. He hunted big game in India as well as on tours of Africa, but most of all, he enjoyed partridge and waterfowl shoots which were organised in regal style. A great angler, he had a vast collection of fishing gear. His fondness for hunting almost cost him his career in sports as he was suspended for having skipped an important match, having preferred to go on a shoot. However, the disaster was averted in time and the suspension was revoked.

In one of its issues brought out on the birth anniversary of K.D. Singh Babu, a Delhi-based institution, Hockey Citizen Group, succinctly glorified him thus:

> *Years ago, there was a hockey player who used to create magic with his hockey stick! Legend has it that this one player was equivalent to twenty-two on the field. The famous hockey player was no one other than Kunwar Digvijay Singh, popularly known as 'Babu'. This great player brought many laurels for the country and unearthed many sporting talents in the country. His individual game and leadership qualities at the Helsinki Olympics brought him global recognition. After retirement from international hockey, Babu helped hockey flourish in India. He launched many innovative schemes to spot and groom sporting talents, especially from schools.*

What the historians of Hockey Citizen Group wrote is not an exaggeration but factual truth. In this biography I have made every effort to put together all events of K.D. Singh Babu's life in a narrative story form, and am quite sure that readers would not only find it very interesting but may even hotly debate as to whether he stepped into the shoes of the great Dhyan Chand or wore shoes a size larger.

My First Reminiscence
Barabanki, August, 1952

If Babu had been the captain of a victorious foreign Olympic team, perhaps some of us would have rushed to do him honour.

—K.M. Munshi, governor of Uttar Pradesh, at a grand reception at Barabanki

It was sometime in August 1952 at our ancestral house in Barabanki that I happened to be a witness to a great victory celebration in honour of my uncle, K.D. Singh Babu. I was just a six-year-old lad then and I had gone with my parents from Lucknow to Barabanki to be there on that glorious day. In very simple terms, we the youngsters were made to understand that uncle had just won the world. In what way it was not easy for us to understand, but there was pandemonium all around. All the family members and friends and admirers from far and wide had gathered at our palatial house for the grand welcome that was being accorded to him. The whole compound was packed to the last inch. The ladies of the family and all us youngsters were made to watch the celebration from the top of the portico. The ladies of the family were showering flowers, coins and sugar candies from the top of the portico, a common sight on auspicious occasions in India's hinterland. A family friend, R.P. Shukla, who was a burly 6'3" giant of a man, had lifted uncle on his shoulders and one could hardly see uncle's face as he was smothered with garlands. There was a whole lot of rejoicing. It appeared as if the whole town had descended on our house and there was a lot of pushing around among the guests. Everyone present wanted a ringside view.

K.D. Singh Babu was a man who knew no social bindings. He would mix well with the high and the mighty of the society as well as with the man on the street. He grew up in this town, sharing ties of sweet intimacy with people from all walks of life, rich and poor, old and young. So it was only natural that when a local hero had come back home as a world champion, people were swarming the house's compound and streets like bees. Sweetmeats were being offered to all to celebrate the most honourable day in the tinsel town of Barabanki.

All that I remember is that a jeep entered the compound and it was being driven by the District Magistrate (DM) of Barabanki, K.A.P. Stevenson, and sitting by his side was the governor of Uttar Pradesh, His Excellency Shri K.M. Munshi.

After the crowd had paid due respect to the two dignitaries, K.D. Singh Babu and R.S. Gentle who had accompanied him to Barabanki, were asked to climb into the jeep to be taken for a victory march to the police lines. They stood flanking the governor while the DM took the wheels. The moment the jeep was about to roll out, someone from the crowd yelled, 'Babubhaiya wah, tumne kamal kar diya!' (Hey brother Babu, you have done wonders). The man who spoke was a rickshaw puller of Barabanki, named Ghoora. The moment K.D. Singh Babu saw him, he jumped down from the jeep and embraced him. The DM and His Excellency watched the scene with great amusement, but for the local people it was nothing new.

Ghoora, I am told, was his assistant when K.D. Singh Babu used to practice solo on the municipal grounds of Barabanki. Bricks would be strategically placed in the field representing imaginary players at various positions and then Ghoora would throw the ball, either from the sideline as if it were passed by the outside-right or from the back. K.D. Singh Babu would collect the ball and then dribble through the laid out bricks to reach the goal. He used to practice for hours on end and Ghoora, not caring for his livelihood, would always be there on time to assist a future star who he believed would one day be acclaimed as the greatest hockey player of the world. When K.D. Singh Babu embraced Ghoora that day, he was acknowledging the contribution of a great assistant.

The very next moment the convoy moved towards the police lines through the narrow streets of Barabanki flooded by admirers, some of who had travelled great distances to witness the victory procession. Barabanki had suddenly catapulted onto the national scene.

In the carefully preserved newspaper clippings of his glorious days, I came across a letter issued by His Excellency the governor of Uttar Pradesh Shri K.M. Munshi issued for the general public dated 15 September 1952 from Raj Bhawan. In this letter, His Excellency had narrated what he saw on that memorable day. It reads as follows:

> *Dear Young Friend,*
>
> *Uttar Pradesh has added another feather to its cap. Babu, the captain of the Indian hockey team which won laurels at the Olympic Games at Helsinki, comes from Barabanki, a small town a few miles from here. He was a student of Lucknow University. I met him as well as Gentle, the left half-back, who earned for himself the reputation of anything but gentle.*
>
> *A governor is expected to know all about games which he has never played and can never understand. So I had an illuminating discussion on hockey.*
>
> *Babu comes from a family of sportsmen; most of his brothers are excellent sportsmen. His six-year-old son is already making headway in hockey. I met them all when I attended a civic reception [given] to Babu at Barabanki, when the whole town had turned out to do him honour, shouting in noisy rhythm 'Babu Babu'.*
>
> *Unlucky for us, the town has only one main street. So [we] went through it in a garlanded jeep from end to end like demi-gods, a military band playing in front of us. But we had to return by the same way through the same crowd like ordinary mortals.*
>
> *These young men told me about the receptions that they had in some parts of Europe as conquering heroes. Naturally, they contrasted them with the utter indifference of our countrymen. No doubt the President received them, and so did the Prime Minister, but our general indifference scarcely did credit to our corporations and universities. If Babu had been the captain of a victorious foreign Olympic team, perhaps some of our people would have rushed to do him honour.*

After that momentous August day of 1952, I only occasionally saw him in action making an appearance in some local exhibition matches, and all that I remember faintly is that he was always the centre of attraction. Then in 1962, I had my first close association with him on the field when a cricket coaching camp was organised at the Central Sports Stadium which is now known as K.D. Singh Babu Stadium in his honour. Sports Officer, Shri Prithvi Raj, an excellent cricketer, was the coach. I and his elder son, Commander, who had given up hockey and was concentrating on cricket, joined the camp. We were just out of high school. While we were attending the cricket camp, K.D. Singh Babu used to hold a hockey training camp by the side.

Both the camps started early at 5 in the morning. He would occasionally come and see us being coached by Shri Prithvi Raj. As a matter of routine, we would come and crowd around the nets and wait for our turns to bat or bowl which took priority over fielding. After watching the camp for a few days, one day, he walked over to our coach and said, 'Sir, please see that your trainees are put through a vigorous exercise for half an hour before they come to the nets.' From the next day on, he saw to it that all us trainees from both hockey and cricket camps were made to run, making rounds of the stadium and then up and down the stairs of the spectator stands, till we got exhausted. It was only after this preliminary that we were allowed to go to the nets.

K.D. Singh Babu always addressed Mr Prithvi Raj as 'Sir' though Mr Raj was his subordinate. When one day, Mr Prithvi Raj humbly protested over this, he smiled and said, 'No Sir, I will always address you as such because I am also learning from you.' It had become a regular feature for him to attend cricket coaching under the watchful eyes of Mr Prithvi Raj. One day, he walked into the nets wearing shorts and holding a hockey stick in hand and requested Mr Prithvi Raj to line up his fast bowlers, which also included his son, Commander. Wearing only the abdominal guards and without pads, he stood in front of the wickets with a hockey stick and challenged them to clean bowl him. It was a big challenge for the fast bowlers and Mr Prithvi Raj too. All of them took chances and it was amazing to see him deflect every ball with the stick. The spinners were also given the same treatment. Challenge over, he gave out a hearty laugh and told us that the trick was to watch and read the ball right from the moment it was released by the bowler. That was the day I realized what made him a great sportsman. He was always prepared to accept challenges and to learn from others.

An interesting participant of the camp was his pet, Neeli. She was a crossbred chocolate-and-white specimen who could best be described as somewhat resembling a springer spaniel. She was gifted to him by Mr K.K. Das, ICS, who was Commissioner of Lucknow at that time. While we boys were learning to play cricket and hockey, Neeli was getting lessons on how to fetch balls on the sidelines of the camps. The immediate purpose was to train her to fetch birds during wildfowl and partridge shoots. Also, waiting for him somewhere in the stadium would be Ustad Rahmatulla, a master craftsman of fishing rods. Thus, right from early morning, his whole day would be spent paying attention to sports activity at all levels while keeping an eye on his hobbies too. That was K.D. Singh Babu—the most versatile personality that I have ever come across in my life.

The ancestral house at Barabanki where K.D. Singh 'Babu' was born.

On the mighty shoulders of R.P. Shukla at the ancestral house just before a civic reception. R.S. Gentle can be seen on right bottom.

Victory procession in Barabanki, 1952. His Excellency, The Governor of Uttar Pradesh Shri K M Munshi seated in the front. Also seen is R.S. Gentle at the back.

K D Singh 'Babu' with the Queen of Uganda. R.S. Gentle, his closest friend on his left.

Team of London Olympics, 1948. Kishen Lal, captain seated in the centre. K.D. Singh 'Babu' seated second from right. By his side is R.S. Gentle.

Examining a hockey stick in a London sports shop, 1948.

Examining hockey sticks being gifted to Indian Team in a London shop, 1948.

The 1947 IHF Team that toured East Africa under the captainship of Major Dhyan Chand. Major Dhyan Chand seated third from left. K.D. Singh 'Babu' standing just behind him.

Autographing a hockey stick for a fan in a London sports shop, 1948.

Examining a 12 bore gun in a London arms shop.

Receiving the gold medal at Helsinki, Finland, 1952.

Toss against Holland in the finals at 1952 Helsinki Olympics.
K.D. Singh 'Babu' played bare feet.

De-boarding at Amsterdam Airport.
Wearing his favourite felt hat.

Kissing the hand of former Miss Finland
after victory at Helsinki.

The victorious Indian Hockey Team with Prime Minister Nehru. The PM is flanked by K.D. Singh 'Babu' and his vice captain Balbir Singh Sr.

The Victorious Indian Hockey Team.

Helms World Trophy. His name is mentioned on top left.

Receiving the Helms World Trophy from former President Dr Rajendra Prasad at Rasthrapati Bhawan, 1953.

Explaining a crucial point to President Dr. Rajendra Prasad at Rasthrapati Bhawan.

With former Chief Secretary of Uttar Pradesh Shri K.K. Das, ICS on a tiger shoot.

Fishing in Ramganga rapids.

With Raja Dinesh Pratap Singh of Kasmanada. Good Mahaseer catch.

Posing with a huge tiger that he shot.

K.D. Singh 'Babu' with a pair of cattle lifters that he shot within split seconds in Aonlakhera, Haldwani.

K.D. Singh 'Babu' with Swamp Deer's that he shot in North Kheri Division.

Evaluating a rifle in his office at Lucknow. Major Dhyan Chand looks on.

With former President Dr. Zakir Hussain.

Donating his both the Olympic gold medals to Shri C.B. Gupta, former Chief Minister o
Uttar Pradesh towards war fund during the Chinese aggression, 1962.

Showing his football skills on the sidelines of Munich Olympics, 1972.

Imparting training to 1972 Munich Olympic team at Lucknow, 1972.

K.D. Singh 'Babu' with a Zebra that he shot in Kenya in 1947. He put up this Zebra in a thicket to attract a lion and sat all night in a Jeep with Major Dhyan Chand to shoot the feline but the lion did not turn up..

K.D. Singh 'Babu' with local shikaris in Kenya.

Kr Naresh Singh, elder brother of K.D. Singh 'Babu' with three sloth bears. He was a tough and hard hitting full back and missed the Olympics due to war.

Early Days

He does not know how to play hockey.

—A sixteen-year-old K.D. Singh Babu about Mohammed Hussain, former Olympian and team member of Dhyan Chand's 1936 Olympic team

My grandfather, Rai Bahadur Thakur Raghunath Singh, was a very distinguished barrister of Barabanki district. Though he inherited sufficient land holding as a landlord and could have led a very comfortable life, he had a very different outlook and always aimed to be ahead of time. Sport and hunting were his favourite pastimes and it is from him that the whole family acquired a liking for both. He was an avid tennis player too. On weekends in the winters, the family would move out of Barabanki and tents would be pegged near a lake for duck shoots. Summers were always spent in Nainital. Since Rai Bahadur sahib had a fairly large family, it required booking of an entire bogey to accommodate eleven children and as many servants, one for each child. A couple of cooks always accompanied the entourage.

The layout of our house at Barabanki stands testimony to the fine lifestyle of Rai Bahadur sahib. A small stable and a fairly big cowshed occupy the rear of the house. Every day, Rai Bahadur sahib would get up at 5 in the morning and after morning prayers at the family temple, one that is built in one of the courtyards of the house, he would attend to the cows and the huge stallion which was the talk of the town. This stallion was an enormous beast and it had the strength required to pull a very heavily loaded carriage. At times, Rai Bahadur sahib would take the reins in his hands and steer the buggy himself to the delight of onlookers.

After the day's work, he would go for a game of tennis in White Club and in the evenings, close friends would regularly assemble at the house for dinner. He never dined alone. After hours of discussion on various issues, the menu would finally be decided by consent of all present. His cook was trained to prepare a range of dishes in rich Kashmiri cuisine. Among his most famous and illustrious friends were Dr Rai Rajeshwar Bali, the taluqdar of Rampur-Daryabad state who was Minister of Education from 1920–1924 and Barrister Bisheshwar Nath, who later on distinguished himself as the first Indian to be elevated to the chair of Chief Judge of Allahabad High Court in 1936.

Let me recount a very interesting story relating to the appointment of Rai Rajeshwar Bali as a minister during the British rule.

Once when Rai Bahadur sahib, who was honoured with this title when he donated a sum of 1 lakh to the government towards war funds (World War I), went to see the collector of Barabanki for some work, the collector made him sit and wait outside his office. Annoyed and disgusted, Rai Bahadur sahib left the office without meeting him. It was a great insult to a person who had helped the government with such a massive amount. No sooner had Rai Rajeshwar Bali assumed office as a minister in 1920, than the two of them decided to teach the collector a lesson. It was decided that the minister would ask the collector to meet him at the house of Rai Bahadur sahib when he arrives at Barabanki. Not intending to cause him too much humiliation, it was decided that some sort of arrangement be made outside the house to seat him. A bangalia (a quadrangle-shaped tiled hutment) was hastily erected at the entrance of the house. On the day of the appointed meeting, the minister arrived early and went straightaway into the drawing room of the house. When the collector arrived, he was asked to sit in the hutment and wait to be called. It was a hot summer day and the collector was naturally getting somewhat uncomfortable. After making him wait for about half an hour, the two friends walked out of the drawing room. The collector greeted the minister and asked for instructions.

'No, there is nothing that I can ask of you,' replied the minister.

Unnerved by this reply, the collector then asked as to why he was summoned.

'Well,' said Rai Rajeshwar Bali, 'this is a return gift to you for the way you made my friend wait outside your office sometime back.'

The hutment is still there and even today it is used to receive visitors.

The foundation of our house was laid in the year 1904 and it was completed by 1911. The built-up area covers a massive 20,000 square feet. It is a palatial house still standing in all its grandeur and during Rai Bahadur sahib's time, it was famed to send out vibrations of nobility. It was in this house that K.D. Singh Babu was born on 22 February 1922; it is here where he grew up acquiring all the qualities of his father.

The house provided all types of surfaces: brick-laid broad pathway, grass turf and bare earth. It was the first playground. Of the six brothers, the eldest never played any game nor did he indulge in hunting but for the other five brothers, games and hunting were routine. After school hours, it was nothing but play. The whole house would reverberate with shouts and the greatest sufferers were the plants and window panes. Almost everything was smashed and the greatest damage was borne by the garage gate which served as one of the goal posts. K.D. Singh Babu was the most talented of all the brothers and whenever others did not join him for games, he would play all alone. He got his first hockey stick at the age of three. He even slept with the stick and ball and not once did he forget to carry both to school.

THE FIRST STEP TO EXHIBITION HOCKEY

Self-trained at home and with friendly matches at school, K.D. Singh Babu started showing signs of a future star from the very beginning. The playgrounds of Government College, Barabanki, laid the foundation for a bright future. He caught the attention of the teachers with his magical stick work and understanding of the game of hockey. Though hockey was his chosen game, he was equally good in football, cricket, tennis and badminton. In the year 1935, when he was just thirteen, he played his first exhibition hockey match with the adults at the Dewa fair. Dewa is a suburb of Barabanki famous for the Sufi saint in whose honour and memory a fair is held every year till today. Exhibition hockey was one of the biggest attractions of the fair at that time and a huge crowd always assembled to watch the keenly contested matches. Despite the pressure of playing before a massive gathering, he showed his class and mastery. From then on there was no looking back and he grew from strength to strength, mastering the skills to perfection. It was often said that he would practice and dribble all alone on the streets of Barabanki for hours. As he continued to practice more and more on varying surfaces, the ball became inseparable from the stick.

DISCOVERY OF K.D. SINGH BABU

Mushfiq-ur-Zaman was a very keen hockey enthusiast of that time. He owned a hotel in Aminabad and all through the year, his one-point programme was to look for talent in hockey. He was a good hockey player and had a keen eye to spot promising players. His sole motive was to pick talented players and then fine-tune their talent. Riding a bicycle, he would visit all playgrounds in Lucknow and even travelled outstation to watch good matches. On one such visit to Shahjahanpur, a district west of Lucknow, he saw young K.D. Singh Babu playing in some inter-collegiate match. The year was 1936 and K.D. Singh Babu was just fourteen years of age. In the match, he was assigned left-half position by the seniors of the team. Mushfiq-ur-Zaman watched keenly and immediately set eyes on him. He found what he was looking for. The next step was a visit to Barabanki. K.D. Singh Babu and his three elder brothers who were also very good hockey players of their time were immediately taken under command and thereafter started lengthy coaching sessions.

Though K.D. Singh Babu used to play as a left-half, it was Mushfiq-ur-Zaman who first saw that he had the potential to excel in the forward position. He started grooming him as an inside-right. Credit is owed to Mushfiq-ur-Zaman for having detected a 'superstar' who would one day completely dominate the game and whom his foes would fear. Even Dhyan Chand at some point had mentioned that the most dangerous position in hockey is inside-right, and showcasing how K.D. Singh Babu proved this is the main meat of this book.

HE DOES NOT KNOW HOW TO PLAY HOCKEY

In the year 1938, K.D. Singh Babu got his first chance to show up at a national level championship. He was only sixteen, and he and his three elder brothers, Kr Bhupendra Singh 'Ramesh', Kr Shukdeo Singh 'Mohan' and Kr Naresh Singh 'Raja' were representing Lucknow Young Men's Association team at the Trades Cup Championship being held in Delhi. Mushfiq-ur-Zaman was the coach and manager of the team. Within two years after he had first spotted K.D. Singh Babu, Mushfiq-ur-Zaman groomed him well as an inside-right. In the first match, LYA. was pitted against a national side by the name of Manavdar Eleven which had many star players including the Olympic full-back, Mohammed Hussain. This full-back had earned the name of 'Wall of China' as it was hard to pass him. He was rather stoutly built and was a ferocious tackler. He had every technique to clear the ball and his presence on the field was enough to demoralise any forward line player.

The highlights of the game were best narrated by his two elder brothers who were playing with him in articles published in the sports annual of the *K.D. Singh Babu Memorial Society* magazine issue of 1981, being reproduced verbatim here. His elder brother, Kr Shukdeo Singh 'Mohan', narrates:

> *I very well remember the first tournament Babu played when our club, the LYA entered the Trades Cup Championship, in New Delhi in 1938. We played against Manavdar Eleven, and Babu as an inside-right was pitted against the left full-back of Manavadar Eleven team, Mohammed Hussain, an Olympic player. It was rightly felt by our talented and inimitable coach—the only one that Babu ever had—that Babu had to be kept ignorant of the identity of the opposite Olympic full-back he was facing, till after the match was over, in order that Babu may play his normal game without any possible psychological inhibition of a well-known name at that time in the hockey world. And of course, Mushfiq-ur-Zaman was confident that his protégé was moulded in purest gold and would shed his brilliance. And that is what actually happened. Babu played a brilliant game—[he] played it with cool confidence, dribbled past left and right of the Olympic stalwart, combined with Irshad on the right flank and with me in the left, in position with masterly precision, which helped him put his first step on the first rung of the ladder of his hockey career which ultimately catapulted him to the top.*

His other brother Kr Naresh Singh 'Raja' described the match in these words:

> *In the presence of a huge crowd witnessing a major tournament, it was no joke for such a young and raw youth to maintain his calm and composure. Further, he had to penetrate the citadel of Mohammed Hussain. In the beginning, when Babu took control of the ball, he would move quickly and before encountering Mohammed Hussain, he would give a pass as told by the coach. Then once he took the ball, he went past the left-half Mohammed Hussain with his fine dribbling and gave a pass to the inside-left. The public stood up and roared in thunderous applause. Mohammed Hussain was beaten not only this time but several times in the match. It was too much for an Olympic player to face such a defeat at the hands of a raw youth, barely sixteen years old. He then decided to ignore Babu's passes and thought of stopping Babu every time that he tried to dodge past him. In the next move, Babu gave a body swerve and gave indications that he would cut through*

> *Mohammed Hussain's right side. It was natural that the Olympic stalwart stretched to the right but Babu had planned his move and he suddenly turned and hurriedly went past the left side. This deceit so unbalanced the Olympian that he fell on the ground. The crowd again roared in applause. Mohammed Hussain fell down twice in trying to tackle Babu as he had no answer. After the final whistle, the whole crowd rushed and lifted Babu and roared like hundred lions and all the while, Mushfiq sahib was seen wiping his tears of joy. Obviously, it was his own glory reflected in Babu. When Mushfiq-ur-Zaman asked his young trainee how could he do all that to the great Olympian, the sixteen-year-old's reply was very simple: 'He does not how to play hockey.' A 'superstar' was born and Mohammed Hussain's career had come to end at the hands of a sixteen-year-old lad.*

Manavdar Eleven was one of the top teams at that time. It was sponsored by the Nawab of Manavdar which was a princely state in Gujarat. The Nawab himself was a good hockey and cricket player and he used to send his team on foreign tours. Mohammed Hussain was its captain and other noted players of the team were Shahbuddin and Peter Fernandes who were incidentally also members of Dhyan Chand's gold medal-winning team at the 1936 Berlin Olympics. Writing for *The Times of India*, Krishna Datta described Mohammed Hussain as a reliable full-back, a stout defender and a 'wall' in the defense. As captain of Manavdar Eleven, he had a successful tour of New Zealand in 1938 but little did he know that back home there was a surprise in store. That same year, a young star by the name of K.D. Singh Babu was about to tell him how to play hockey.

Hockey, All in the Family

Had war not intervened [in the] holding of [the] 1940 and 1944 Olympics, all four brothers would surely have been selected in the Indian Olympic side.

—Dr A.C. Chaterjee, Secretary, Indian Hockey Federation 1937–1945, as quoted in K.D. Singh Babu Memorial Society Magazine, 1981

With the annexation of Austria in 1938 by Germany, war clouds loomed large over Europe. Consequently no Olympic Games were held in 1940. This came as a big shock for the hockey-playing family of K.D. Singh Babu as he and his three elder brothers, Kr Bhupendra Singh 'Ramesh', Kr Shukdeo Singh 'Mohan' and Kr Naresh Singh 'Raja', all of who were inducted in the Uttar Pradesh state hockey team in 1940, were sure to make it to the Olympic side. That would have been a unique distinction—four brothers representing the nation at one time. In an interview given to a Hindi daily *Swatantra Bharat*, on 23 April 1978, Dr A.C. Chaterjee, former president of Lucknow University Athletic Association, who also happened to be secretary of Indian Hockey Federation (IFH) from 1937-1945, said, 'Had war not intervened [in the] holding of [the] 1940 and 1944 Olympics, all the four brothers would have surely been selected for the Olympic side.' The brothers distinguished themselves at various times. While Kr Bhupendra Singh captained the Lucknow University hockey and tennis teams in 1937, Kr Shukdeo Singh rose to become captain of the Uttar Pradesh team in 1944–45. Even the youngest, my father, Dr Kr. Suresh Singh, who was more concerned with his studies, was good enough in the game and he too captained the Lucknow University Hockey Eleven team in the 50s.

By the time the war folded up in 1945, Ramesh and Raja had lost interest in furthering their hockey careers, limiting themselves to only club level matches. However, Kr Shukdeo Singh 'Mohan' continued to move ahead, along with K.D. Singh Babu, and it was said that he was one of the finest inside-lefts of the game at that time. His dribbling and ball control was out of the world and it was said of him that he possessed a terrific reverse flick which became deadly inside the circle as the opposition hardly got any time to readjust and react. Unfortunately, due to amoebic dysentery that he contracted in 1945 and which troubled him for over a year, he gave up playing completely. K.D. Singh Babu, who played under his captaincy, always maintained that he was a complete and better player than him and had fate not spoiled his chances, he was sure to be there in the 1948 Olympic team with a chance to lead. As other brothers sidelined themselves one by one for one reason or the other, only K.D. Singh Babu was left to carry the torch of the family forward.

NEAR END OF A CAREER

Apart from sports, hunting big and small game was a favourite adventure the whole family indulged in. Forest blocks were booked every summer and winter, and the happy hunting grounds were the terai in the foothills of Kumaon. Preparations were made well in advance with a lead party reaching the forest guest house with provisions for an enjoyable fortnight's stay. Though it hurts to say it now, the most contested issue at that time used to be: who will get *a chance to shoot a tiger*? A lottery used to be drawn and the one whose name was picked would get a chance to sit on the machan. A machan is a temporary arrangement of a makeshift cot placed 10–12 feet above the ground on a tree. A hunter, assisted by a helper with a torch, used to sit on it in wait for the tiger to approach the tiger on the previous night.

In the year 1946, a great clash of a future career and hunting expedition took place. K.D. Singh Babu was a star player of the Lucknow University team and all depended on him in the inter-varsity hockey meet of 1945. It was expected that Lucknow University would do well with an inside-right like him. But most unfortunately, the dates of the inter-varsity meet collided with those of a forest shooting block already booked. The temptation to be in the inviting forests along with his brothers for a fortnight of merrymaking and a chance to level the sight of the gun on the elusive tiger was too much of a temptation. Quietly, our star slipped out of town, gave his stick a rest and landed where his mind lay.

No one can say for certain why he took such a decision. Was it that he was not serious about carving a future in hockey or did he just think that the inter-varsity matches were not as important, it is not known. Taken aback by his absence, which they took as misconduct, the university authorities slapped a suspension of one year on him. Preparations for the first post-war Olympics scheduled to be held in the year 1948 were in full swing and rumours were afloat of a team being sent to Sri Lanka (then Ceylon) in the same year, followed by a tour of East Africa under the captainship of Major Dhyan Chand in 1947. Continuation of suspension was sure to ruin a bright career. Disgusted by this action, K.D. Singh Babu lost all interest in hockey and he even retracted from any serious practice. Then, all of a sudden, matters took a turn.

Knowing full well that K.D. Singh Babu was the future of India's hockey, one of his friends, J.N. Chakarvarty, who was captain of the Lucknow University hockey team at that time, approached him to give up his membership of LYA and instead join Bengali Young Men's Association, of which Dr A.C. Chaterjee was the patron. At that time, Dr Chaterjee had a big say in all matters relating to hockey as he was also the secretary of the IHF. Dr Chaterjee had sweet relations with the entire family right from 1937. K.D. Singh Babu joined BYA as advised. Pleased with a star joining his association, Dr Chaterjee then convinced the vice chancellor and president of Lucknow University Hockey Association, Shri S.K. Datta, to revoke the suspension in the interest of the country. It was done forthright and a great disaster was averted. Once again, the stick had replaced the gun.

The Lotus Blooms 1946–1948

It is tempting to write that Babu is as elusive as Dhyan Chand.

—Press report after an exhibition match just before the team was to leave for London Olympics

Babu was the brains of the attack.

—Sports Correspondent Berry Sarbhadhikary from London, Hindustan Times

After the timely escape from the horror of a year-long suspension an opportunity came his way to tour South India and Ceylon in 1946 under the captainship of R.S. Gentle, who later on became a great personal friend. On this tour, he outshone every other player and the press glorified him by writing: '*Babu was the outstanding player as far as stick work is concerned and [our] thoughts go back to the famous Dhyan Chand when he was in action.*'

This tour was an eye-opener for the selectors and reinforced the belief of many who saw in him a future 'superstar'. At that time, K.D. Singh Babu was only twenty-four years old. The press flashed a picture of him in action with a compliment in the caption: 'A Wizard in Action'. He was already being compared to Dhyan Chand. This was followed by a tour of British East Africa in 1947. The IHF got a request from Asia Sports Association to send a top team for exhibition matches, with a special request that the team should be led by Major Dhyan Chand. This tour of East Africa was significant on two counts. First and foremost was the opportunity for younger players to play alongside Dhyan Chand, and secondly, more importantly, this was a preliminary test for the 1948 Olympics selection.

The team was constituted thus:

Dhyan Chand (captain), KishenLal (Bombay), K.D. Singh Babu (UP), Leo Pinto (Bombay), R.C. Francis (Madras), Walter D'Souza (Bombay), R.S. Gentle (Delhi), Keshav Datta (Punjab), M. Vaz (Bombay), P. Jansen (Bengal), Mushtaq Ahmed (Bengal), B. Kapoor (Bengal), Manna Singh (Gwalior), R.J. Kar (Bengal), Gurbachan Singh (Punjab), Rajgopal (Mysore), and L.A. Shakoor (Bhopal).

Significantly, the first nine names mentioned after Dhyan Chand made it to the Olympic side of 1948. The team gave a splendid performance and a total of 270 goals were scored, out of which K.D. Singh Babu scored 70, followed by Dhyan Chand who scored 63 goals. This tour gave K.D. Singh Babu cause for a smile. He proved beyond doubt that India needed him, and an inside-right like him was the answer for future victories. Playing under the watchful eyes of the great wizard was no easy feat. Even though the opposing teams were too weak, the tour was a great success in as much as the nine players who made the larger part of the 1948 Olympic team were able to co-ordinate among themselves, and what could be better than playing alongside Dhyan Chand himself! Now the team was well prepared to face any world opposition.

Although memories of the last mishap whence his career nearly came to an end were still fresh in his mind, hunting was such an obsession with him that on this tour too he looked for an opportunity to shoot a lion. In an interview given to *Swatantra Bharat* in 1978 to recall his days with K.D. Singh Babu soon after the latter's demise, Dhyan Chand fondly narrated an incident from the 1946–47 East Africa tour and said:

> *We drove 300 hundred miles out of Nairobi into a thick forest. Babu shot a couple of gazelles and antelopes. Then late in the evening, he shot a zebra and dragged it into a thicket where he expected the lions to come and feed on the carcass. We sat in an open Land Rover all night, and yet, no lion appeared. It was my first experience of a big game shoot. Some guinea fowl shoots were also organised and K.D. Singh Babu always took great delight in cooking some for me.*

The tour brought K.D. Singh Babu very close to the wizard who was himself by now convinced that someone was finally really stepping into his shoes. Back home, as preparations were being made for the 1948 Olympics with the holding of inter-provincials and exhibition matches, fans and critics started to see in him 'shades of Dhyan Chand', even as some sports writers were very critical of his style of play which they thought was not in line with the interest of the team. This was primarily because by this time in his career, he had developed such magical stick work that he could hold on to the ball as long as he wished. At that time, UP did not have many star players while other teams like the Railways, Customs and Services were star-studded. Keeping in mind that he had no valuable support from his other teammates, he often made UP look like a one-man team.

Undeterred by such comments, he continued to play in his own style and showed to the world of hockey that he had acquired all the rare qualities of a genius. He could make solo runs and score, he could beat the entire defense, and he could feed his forwards with open goals. From then on, he was a man with a mission. Even when his side lost, he stole the limelight and the press always came out in praise of his game.

During the East Africa tour, K.D. Singh Babu fell ill and was hospitalised for a long time back in India. However, he continued to participate in various tournaments. Leading a weak UP side in the Beighton Cup held in Calcutta in 1948, UP reached the finals owing to his brilliant game. After the finals against the Port Commissioners, the press wrote:

> *Babu, who was an outstanding success in the Indian team's tour of East Africa under the captaincy of Dhyan Chand, showed splendid stick work. He was a constant source of danger to the local defense. In Babu UP had a meritorious forward who provided a problem for the Port defense. The brilliant goal scored by him which incidentally gave his side the equaliser was a [striking] feature of the match. The Port defenders had to resort to desperate methods including body play to stop him. In the minute before the interval, Babu broke the Port defense by tricking two defenders in fine style and scored with a brilliant angular shot which left the Port goalie guessing.*

The criticism repeated off and on that at times he did not keep in mind the interest of the team was totally unfounded. Many a times when his teammates failed to match up to expectations, he had no choice but to take chances and make solo efforts.

The Beighton Cup was followed by the Nationals which were being held at Bombay Gymkhana. Though UP were the joint holders of the Beighton Cup, they put up a bad show and were eliminated by Mysore. However, the press wrote:

> *Mysore were never expected to beat UP, specially as the losers had the redoubtable Babu in their ranks, and all were disappointed by their display.*

> *Babu, India's greatest inside-right at the moment, played a lone hand in the UP attack with the result that he could do little to make an impression on those who watched [him] in action today. Besides, it is believed that Babu is not keeping good health after his recent tour of East Africa and [going] by his display we saw, we were apt to believe this, as it was a tame Babu and not the same player we saw in action for the IHF before the side left for Africa.*

Despite not keeping well, he continued to give outstanding performances. Not only was a selection in the Olympic Eleven seen as only quite natural but he was also seen as a forward who was supposed to play the pivotal role at the coming 1948 Olympics. All eyes were focused on him as he had totally eclipsed Dhyan Chand during the East Africa tour. In preparation for the Olympics, the IHF selected a team of probables and the team was made to play exhibition matches in Bombay and Madras which was basically to work out various combinations. In every match, young K.D. Singh Babu was the centre of attraction and appreciation. He silenced his critics not only by his grand display but even proved the point as to why he often held on to the ball for long periods of time. The exhibition matches put him in the driving seat and match after match, every report that followed clearly showed that he was the player to be watched at the coming Olympics. Comparing him to Dhyan Chand, a critic wrote:

> *India's Olympic representatives were seen in action for the second time on Sunday in exhibition hockey matches at the Cooperage and their performance was worthy of a team of international players.*
>
> *It was not a great display, not by a long stretch, but a fast-moving clever attack in which Babu was an outstanding success who knew the secret of getting goals. It is tempting to write that Babu is as elusive as Dhyan Chand. I am content to say that India is lucky to have such a brilliant forward in the team. He is a complete answer to any selector's prayer. Babu dominated the scene and scored two "picture goals", dazzling a host of defenders in the process of doing so.*

In yet another match against Bombay Eleven which the India side won by 5–1, the press wrote:

> *It was a disappointing display where the question of team work was concerned as a number of players were still inclined to forget what they have been taught and were apt to overdo the frills.*

Noting that the exhibition was pathetic, it further said:

> *Babu was without question the most dangerous of the India forwards today and three of the five goals came of his stick. Two were from practically solo efforts, the last of the day coming after he beat a number of defenders on his own. But the best was his first, from a corner award. Stopping the ball on the reverse, he got into position and shot into an empty gap, all within a couple of seconds.*

In the eyes of the critics, this India team was still short of pulling up a miracle. In exhibition matches that the team played against an Anglo-Indian Eleven and Madras Eleven at Madras, the critics came down heavily on the capability of various players but continued to single out K.D. Singh Babu for his praiseworthy game. In the first exhibition match against Anglo-Indian Eleven, the Indian hockey team were trailing by 2–0 till fifteen minutes from end. The ground at Madras Cricket Club was too fast a surface and the Anglo-Indians gave India's representative side a lot of reasons to worry. One newspaper report summed it up thus:

> *The India representatives were disappointing—at any rate they played below expectations—in the first half, during which they seldom, if ever, showed that finesse and supreme stick work of previous Olympic teams. And certainly they did nothing to confirm the general belief that they would retain India's title at London.*

From such criticism it was apparent that no one saw any good prospects for India and the country's only hope was K.D. Singh Babu. The report further added:

> *But if there is any forward who can be compared with the Dhyan Chand - Roop Singh class, it is Babu, the inside-right. Endowed with remarkable stick work and speed, he outshone every other forward.*

The India representatives then played two matches against Madras Eleven and in both matches, it was K.D. Singh Babu who mattered. The critics were still of the opinion that India hardly stood a chance to retain the gold; save for K.D. Singh Babu, no other team member showed any class. Commenting after the first match against Madras Eleven, the press wrote:

> *The India team, no doubt, gave an improved display but not convincing enough to confirm the general belief that they would prove worthy successors to the previous Indian world-beaters.*

Then, again singling out K.D. Singh Babu, it added:

> *Once again, Babu proved to be the cleverest of India forwards. Time and again, he ripped wide open the Madras defense with his fine body swerve and stick work, and one of the three goals that he scored was a gem. Picking up a loose ball in midfield, he was through in a flash, beating two defenders in the twinkling of an eye and crowning a really grand effort with a beautiful drive.*

In the subsequent match played against the same Madras side, he again mesmerised the opponents and brought much joy to the spectators. Describing the match, a hockey correspondent wrote:

> *On a conservative reckoning, the Olympic team missed at least half a dozen glorious scoring chances before they actually opened their account in the twenty-fifth minute. Then outside-left, Latif, bringing down a ball in the air, left Richtor standing to race down the flank and send across a reverse centre of outstanding power and accuracy. Babu positioned just inside the "D" did the rest, the strength behind his effort carrying the ball through the net.*
>
> *Three more goals followed in a hectic five-minute spell after the change of ends. Latif, after a lightning-like burst, improved the position and then Babu brought much joy to the spectator's hearts with a gem of an effort and one that forcibly reminded them of the days when hockey forwards were reckoned purely and simply on their wizardry with the stick.*

Describing yet another goal that he scored, the press called it a 'peach of an effort' and described it thus:

> *Obtaining possession some forty yards out, Babu had three defenders between him and his objective, including the goalkeeper. He dazzled the first effortlessly, telegraphed his intentions before making a victim of the next, and finally left the goalkeeper aghast. It was a peach of an effort and a few minutes later, Babu added his second goal and the team's fourth.*

Thereafter, in the last match that the India representatives played against Maharasthra Eleven, it became more than evident that he had hardly any good support from his teammates and most often had to rely on his own game and scheming. Covering this match, a correspondent wrote:

> *The visitors from Maharashtra proved quite a handful for the formidable Indian Eleven in the second match of the evening and only the brilliance of Babu and a magnificent goal by Latif influenced the issue in favour of India's representative side. Babu, India's sleek-as-silk inside-right was the best*

forward on view but with little support coming from his colleagues on either side of him, he was compelled to play a lone hand. Even then he exposed the limitations of Maharashtra's defenders and often threatened to score.

So even before the team left for the London Olympics, K.D. Singh Babu was already being compared to the wizard, the legendary Dhyan Chand. In the eyes of critics and fans, he was a meritorious forward and the greatest inside-right in the country at that moment. Dhyan Chand was often quoted as saying that inside-right is the most dangerous position in the game of hockey. So at the London Olympics, everything depended on him. The big game hunter was most often left to hunt by himself and no wonder the Indian spectators at the London Olympics, who had heard stories of his exploits in East Africa and pre-Olympic matches back in India, were always heard shouting, 'Babu, Babu, come on Babu', for he was their hope of an Indian victory.

The performance of Dhyan Chand and Roop Singh, his younger brother, at the Berlin Olympics of 1936 was the last impression that the critics carried as an indelible mark of the standard of the game that was set by that team and no one could visualise a repeat performance of that feat. It was no surprise that in 1948 too, parallels were still being drawn with the 1936 Olympic team. The so-called Hitler-Dhyan Chand episode of 1936 was still fresh in mind and no one worth their name in hockey circles thought of a chance for India to emerge at the top.

Simultaneously, at the centre of criticism and appreciation was K.D. Singh Babu. The partition of the sub-continent into India and Pakistan and the migration of some good English players back to England had created further problems for the selectors. For the final formation, names were being added and deleted.

While the team was being finalised, some sports critics were casting doubts on the ability of the team so far as harmony was concerned. Comments were bandied about that this team had to play as a unit like the Penningers Amsterdam team of 1928 and Lal Shah Bokhari's team of Los Angeles of 1932. N.N. Mukherjee was the official coach of the 1948 team. Various press write-ups reported that team work is what Mukherjee was struggling for and that although most players were modelling their game on the trainer's advice, a few still appeared determined to defeat his plans. By using the words 'a few', the finger was actually pointed at K.D. Singh Babu who was seen as playing to the gallery and not playing in the interest of the team and the country. One sport critic writing by the name of Argus added:

> *I hate to say so, but that brilliant player, Babu, is one of them. In previous hockey teams, India has had better dribblers than Babu is ever likely to be. Dhyan Chand could safely be called the king of the dribble, with Roop Singh running a close second. Between them these famous brothers could run through half a dozen sides, leave alone one. But did Dhyan Chand indulge in frills? Even on the recent East Africa tour, he advised players against pattern weaving and Babu was one of his colleagues on the trip. Incidentally, Babu is a player of a province made famous by Dhyan Chand and Roop Singh and he has only to pattern his game on the style of the famous brothers to contribute another colourful chapter to India's hockey glory.*

From the foregoing it had become crystal clear that the critics were also of the view that at the 1948 Olympics, all depended on this great inside-right if India were to retain the Olympic gold. It was a piquant situation. Criticism and expectation played out side by side. While criticising his style of play, little did anyone understand that quite often he had to resort to solo run-ups as his teammates failed to respond to his match-making moves. He had already distinguished himself as a master strategist and the chief playmaker around whom the whole team revolved. He had the marksman's ability to find suitably positioned teammates he had the jugglery to pass through a maze of panicky defenders and he could show results on demand.

A fortnight before the team was to leave for London, tragedy struck the team. Udham Singh, selected to play as a centre-forward, injured his fingers. Coach Mukherjee spoke in glowing terms of this centre-forward but the doctors ruled him out. This put the selectors in a dilemma and they considered Shakoor of Bhopal or Glacken of Bengal as a replacement. Ultimately, it was Glacken who made it and at the last minute, Balbir Singh Sr, R.S. Gentle and Leslie Claudius were also included in the team. Udham Singh's misfortune became a boon for Balbir Singh Sr as the other centre-forward Glacken, who was at that time considered as an ideal replacement for Udham Singh, remained out of form and was rested after a few matches.

Burdened with last minute changes, controversies and criticism, the team from Independent India finally left for London in August 1948 under the captainship of Kishen Lal, the right-out who, incidentally, had also played for Jhansi, the town of Dhyan Chand and later on had represented Bombay. Expectations ran high. Being compared to the great

Dhyan Chand during the pre-Olympic exhibition games at Bombay put extra pressure on K.D. Singh Babu. It was a real testing time; it was time to show that he had really stepped into the shoes of the wizard. All eyes were focused on him and moreover, he had to silence his critics. The Indian residents of London had already heard about his superb display during the East Africa tour under Dhyan Chand and they turned out in large numbers to see the new wizard in action. Could India do it again? His teammates knew his capabilities and they voted him vice-captain. One press note said:

> *Our Indian hockey team has the heavy responsibility of retaining the Olympic championship we have held since we first took part in the world games. It is a star-studded side, but playing under conditions suitable for heavier teams like Britain, our representatives have a stiffer task than on previous conditions. Playing against Pakistan, they will have to put their best foot forward for it will be a case of Greek meeting Greek.*

It was the first time that the press accepted the fact that conditions during the 1948 Olympics were far different from those during the previous Olympics when the opposing teams were not up to the mark and India had easy runs. During the twelve-year period since the last Olympics of 1936, other nations had fine-tuned their game and by 1948, England, Holland, Germany and Pakistan had become formidable forces in hockey. And there was no Dhyan Chand in the Indian team now. The final selection of twenty players read as follows:

Kishen Lal, Bombay (Captain and Forward), K.D. Singh Babu, UP (Vice-Captain, Inside-right), P. Jansen, Calcutta (Forward), Reg Rodricks, Bombay (Forward), Balbir Singh, Punjab (Forward), Laurie Frenandes, Bombay (Forward), Latif, Bhopal (Outside-left), G. Glacken, Bengal (Forward), Keshav Dutta, Bombay (Centre-half), Leslie Claudius, Bengal (Centre-half), MaElevene Vaz, Bombay (Left-half), Yaswan Rajput, Delhi (Left-half), Amir Kumar, Punjab (Centre-half), Akhtar Hussain, Bhopal (Left Full-back), R.S. Gentle, Bombay (Left Full-back), Trilochan Singh, Faridkot (Right Full-back), Walter D'Souza, Bombay (Right Full-back), R. Francis, Madras (Goalkeeper), Leo Pinto, Bombay (Goalkeeper) and G. Singh Nandy, Punjab (Forward).

1948 OLYMPICS, LONDON

The Indian hockey team finally left for London on 13 July with N.N. Mukherjee as coach and Dr A.C. Chaterjee as manager. Earlier, during the exhibition matches, they had come under heavy fire and most of the critics thought that the team had poor chances of retaining the gold. However, there was only one hope and the critics had made this very clear in their reports after witnessing the exhibition matches—the wizardry of K.D. Singh Babu.

India in Group A had a fairly easy preliminary round, having being grouped with Argentina, Austria and Spain. They convincingly beat Argentina 9–1, and Austria 8–0. These two matches were almost one-sided and the Indian team exploited the dry ground conditions on both occasions. While winning against a weak Austrian side could hardly be touted as a victory of merit, the press in its report of the match referred to K.D. Singh Babu as 'Indian Hockey Idol'. Stories of his wizardry during the East Africa tour under the captaincy of Dhyan Chand were already in circulation and he was the main focus of the spectators, the press and the opponents. The next match was against Spain, which was considered a very weak side. It was expected that India would again beat them by a convincing margin but since the ground conditions were very heavy, they could only register a 2–0 win, one of which was scored by K.D. Singh Babu out of a penalty bully. There is a very interesting incident that happened in the course of this match. The Spaniards had been well advised about his scheming game and they were determined not to allow him to increase the margin of defeat. After the Spaniards were 2 down, K.D. Singh Babu got hold of the ball and made a solo run towards the striking circle. Sensing that he would surely score again, seven of them rushed towards the goal line and stood along the side of the goalkeeper. The remaining four camped out of the ring but within the twenty-five yards. At this moment, K.D. Singh Babu was on top of the circle and seeing the Spaniards grouped tightly, he stopped right there. He teased them from the top of the circle and tried his best to draw them out but the Spaniards refused to leave the goal line. It was the dying moment of the game. Finally, he smiled and gave a back pass to MaElevene Vaz to draw them out, but they refused to stir and risk more goals. Thereafter, the final whistle sounded. India had by now qualified for a semi-final berth and the Spaniards basked in the great relief of being beaten by a low margin. In an article written for *Sports and Pastime* in 1952, K.D. Singh Babu had himself described this incident as the most amusing recollection of his playing days.

In Group B, England topped the table, having put up some splendid show while in Group C, Holland and Pakistan were in a neck-to-neck struggle, both having beaten Belgium, France and Denmark and it was left to the last match to nail the decision as to which semi-final each would play. Pakistan played beautifully in that match and beat Holland 6–1 in a manner that suggested that their players were reaching peak form.

In accordance with Olympic rules, the semi-finals involved England and Pakistan while India was to play Holland. The climax had been set and this is what the IHF had estimated about these four nations reaching the penultimate stage. Both the semi-finals were played the same day in the same venue. The first semi-final was between India and Holland. The team consisted of:

Pinto (Goalkeeper), Trilochan Singh (Right-back), R.S. Gentle (Left-back), Keshav Dutt (Right-half), Amir Kumar (Centre-half), MaElevene Vaz (Left-half), Kishen Lal (Right-out), K.D. Singh (Right-in), G.R. Glacken (Centre-forward), A. Jansen (Left-in) and L. Fernandes (Left-out).

In this semi-final against Holland, Dr A.C. Chaterjee was inclined to play Balbir Singh as centre-forward but K.D. Singh Babu, who, being team vice-captain, had more confidence in Glacken, went up to the dressing room and convinced Dr Chaterjee to play Glacken. He assured him that it was his duty to see that India won the match. Such was his confidence. The ground conditions were very heavy and India and Pakistan were handicapped owing to the sodden state of the ground after the rain over the weekend, but India accustomed themselves more quickly to the conditions than Pakistan.

The semi-final between India and Holland turned out to be what the newspapers called a 'battle of custodians' in which Holland's Richter came out brilliantly. The Dutch goalkeeper was the hero of the match. For long periods, he was the white-capped pivot around whom the game revolved in the Dutch goalmouth. Everyone in the arena appreciated his courage and skill in robbing the fast Indian attack from scoring. Due to sodden ground conditions, K.D. Singh Babu too was playing a defensive game. Holland fought throughout the seventy minutes of play and W. van Heel and R.T. Esser made some magnificent solo moves. Pinto, the Indian goalkeeper, too had to fight hard for some time in the Indian goalmouth and he made some magnificent clearances, but there were long periods when the ball was well away from him. Indians were superior in stick work and dribbling but shooting within the circle was often faulty, particularly by the centre-forward, Glacken. This gave some anElevenous moments to Dr Chaterjee as he was inclined to play Balbir Singh in that position and as it appeared that Glacken was totally out of form. Sensing his anElevenety and taking some time off, K.D. Singh Babu went up to Dr Chaterjee who was seated in the jury box and said to him, 'Do not get worried Dr Sahib, I will just get you what you desire.' The spell of defensive play called for new fire from the Indian attack and no sooner had they swept up the field and opened a movement, than they got the opening goal. The first goal came from Jansen, and an easy one it proved to be. From inside the penalty area, he tapped a light shot to Richter, which the Dutch goalkeeper attempted to clear, but misjudged and the ball trickled over the line into the net.

If not for some uncanny anticipation and interception, India would have got the second goal sooner than it did. But they did get the goal all right, by K.D. Singh Babu, within minutes of the first goal. The press wrote:

> *K.D. Singh had been spurred on by affectionate shouts of "Babu, Babu, come on Babu" from the Indian spectators. It was a well-merited goal. It crashed into the net from top of the circle, leaving the Dutch goalkeeper, Richter, helpless on his knees. The Indian inside-right's score was a combination effort with Glacken and Fernandes who supported him in his magnificent run from well past midfield.*

Since Glacken had missed earlier chances, K.D. Singh Babu did not depend on him this time and saw to it that he fulfilled his promise to Dr Chaterjee. Describing the memorable incident in the 1982 Sports Annual of *K.D. Singh Babu Memorial Society* publication, Dr Chaterjee wrote: 'Apart from scoring a magnificent field goal himself, Babu had a major hand in the first goal too.'

By half time, India was leading, 2–0. Though Holland made several attempts after half-time, Pinto's superb work in the Indian goal robbed them of any chance to reduce the margin. By now India was making the ball move faster with K.D. Singh Babu spearheading the attack, and four times, it looked as if India was going to take a further lead. But every time, the Dutch goalkeeper, Richter, made magnificent clearances. Fernandes, Jansen, Glacken, K.D. Singh Babu and Kishen Lal, each of them made an attempt to beat Richter, but no one could do it. That day, Richter was indomitable. By close of time, Holland's turn came and they were awarded a penalty bully which Bromberg, the Dutch forward, converted. Finally, India let go another chance when Jansen seized a pass inside the striking circle but the hit soared over the crossbar. By this time, the heavy ground was beginning to take its toll and the emerald green field had started to look brown in patches. Ultimately, India trounced Holland, 2–1, and qualified for the finals.

The other semi-final was played on the same ground between England and Pakistan. The British team was led by the very versatile Norman Borrett who was an excellent all-round sportsman. Apart from hockey, he was good in squash and tennis and was also a first-class cricket player. Pakistan was without Mohammed Niaz Khan, their brilliant right-back who had a cut under his right eye. As subsequent events showed, the British team reached the peak of its form in this semi-final. The Olympic Games had opened in bright sunshine on dry flat grounds but the weather had steadily deteriorated into chilly wet conditions with soft and rather slippery turf. British players were well accustomed to these conditions. Britain attacked right from the first bully off and they put Pakistan on the back foot. The game became more rugged with players from both sides using their weight. The light was becoming dull as the first half drew to a close with both teams fighting hard to break the defense of the other. Britain was playing a more open game, but this was not paying dividends because of the greater speed of Pakistan. At the same time, it helped to counter the brilliant stick work of Pakistani players. The second half started with both teams striving hard to obtain a lead. Hamid, Masud, Burki and Shahrukh, all made brilliant efforts but they could not beat the British defense. Shahrukh, the centre-half, brought the crowd to its feet with a splendid run down the left wing. Then, from a short corner, Dara drove hard but the ball flew just too high. In the last quarter of an hour, Pakistan's players did everything but score against a determined and weary British defense. The British players were persistent in their aggressive tactics. A long solo run by Peake on the extreme right swept the ball to his inside-right, White, who crashed it into the Pakistan goal amid tremendous applause from the crowd just twenty minutes from half-time. The initial score electrified the British team and just five minutes later, Adlard, the British centre-forward, put Britain two goals ahead. But the Pakistanis were far from beaten. They rallied hard and drove back the lively British attack. Unfortunately, though, in the closing minutes of the game, their two strong cross drives sailed past the British goalmouth without a score. And so Britain reached the final with two goals to no one.

England-India Final, 12 August 1948

The British team entered the finals with a very impressive card. Till now in all the previous matches they had conceded not even a single goal whereas India had conceded two goals. The British team was full of confidence as the conditions suited them and they were riding high after having dispatched Pakistan who played a game similar to that of the Indians. However, Indian team manager Dr A.C. Chaterjee had prophesied aloud to sports reporters three days earlier, that India would defeat England by at least three goals. And India did one better by making it 4–0 when the match ended.

Writing exclusively for *The Statesman*, C.E. Newman narrated it as follows:

> *India today is the undisputed champion of the world in hockey, and her flag floated proudly over the great Wembley Stadium during the victory ceremony. It was a great achievement to win at three successive Olympiads at Amsterdam, Los Angeles and Berlin but the hockey world always felt there was something slightly lacking in the title until it involved beating Britain.*
>
> *The meeting between the world's greatest hockey nations has now taken place for the first time, fittingly enough in an Olympic final and the British team was truly and well beaten. It is an achievement of which India should really be proud. It was a magnificent struggle from beginning to end before a record British crowd of 25,000 between a dogged British defense which had hitherto not conceded a goal and an Indian attack, to the versatility and brilliance of which Britain for the most part could find no reply. Conditions were very much against the Indian tactics, but their players adapted themselves in a manner which deserves the highest praise. The crowd paid the highest tributes to India's great display and the British players said with one voice: "We were well and truly beaten by a better side". It was perhaps not one of the finest displays the world has ever seen, because India's superiority was so marked, but it was a game so memorable that no one is likely to forget it.*

Writing for the Hindustan Times, Berry Sarbadhikary summed it up thus:

> *The merit of the Indian victory was enhanced by the fact that conditions were against them. The turf was too dead to permit swift ground passes which is the backbone of artistic attack. This slowness often compelled an Indian forward to get past a British defender twice. However, within 12 minutes, the Indians were 2–0 up, which broke the back of British determination. However, Brodie, the British goalkeeper, was the man responsible for keeping the Indian tally within limits.*
>
> *The four-goal victory tells its own tale of Indian supremacy in every department of the game. Our forwards were of course [a] quicker and cleverer lot with Babu as the brains of the attack.*
>
> *At half-time, a fine drizzle began to fall. The British looked pleased and the Indians grimaced at the soft turf. However, the Indians did not let the rain discourage them. The light footwear the Indians were using did not make for speed under such conditions, so they took them off. The tally could have been better than 4–0 but Balbir Singh missed two easy chances.*

By far the most scintillating account of the match was given by an NS Special Correspondent who, while headlining his report '*Babu's Performance Was as Near to Perfection as Possible*' wrote:

> *India retained her monopoly in world hockey with an all-round superiority that was even more convincing than her four-goal victory over Great Britain in the finals of the Olympic Championship would show. There was not one of the 20,000 crowd present that did not leave the Empire Stadium completely thrilled with the truly great performance of the Indian side.*
>
> *Rising to unprecedented heights, the Indians completely dominated the exchanges and Britain were indeed fortunate that at the end of seventy minutes of play, they were only four goals in arrears.*
>
> *Though it would be invidious to single out any individual member of the winning side, three players were chiefly instrumental in paving the way for India's brilliant performance. The pick of the bunch were inside-right Babu and half-backs Amir Kumar and MaElevene Vaz.*
>
> *The deep defenders, Trilochan Singh and Gentle, though not in the best of form, did not give Pinto, the goalkeeper, any anElevenety mainly due to the stubborn half-back line. Keshav improved with time but it was the fine positional play and interception and the wide-flung distribution of Amir Kumar and Vaz that enabled India to get on top and remain in that enviable position.*

> *Brilliant as were the performances of these players, inside-right Babu outshone his colleagues with a masterly display of stick work and distribution. Checking his tendency to hang on to the ball, Babu turned in a performance as near perfection as was possible. Scintillating dribbling and adroit through passes characterised his play and he was the chief instigator in completely tying up a dogged England defense.*
>
> *He was well supported by his forwards, who, though capitalizing on all his astute passes, did enough in early stages of the game to knock the fight out of their opponents.*
>
> *Kishen, exploited to the point of monotony, responded with some dazzling spurts but his opposite number, Lawrie Fernandes, was yet to develop the required international temperament. Inside-left Jansen was always dangerous while centre-forward Balbir Singh scored when his side needed it most.*
>
> *In the initial stages, Balbir Singh let the chances go a begging. Babu then had the defenders on the wrong foot and his perfect through pass was converted by the centre-forward.*
>
> *Ultimately, with a four-goal lead, India treated the crowd to an exhibition of short passes but nearly had the mortification of seeing Britain score a goal. Pinto, however, kept his charge intact by coming out to defend a penalty bully awarded against India in the last five minutes of play.*
>
> *Then capping his brilliant performance throughout the game, Babu brought the crowd to its feet with a field-length dribble that left England's defenders bewildered but his drive sailed over the bar a minute before the referee signalled a convincing India victory.*

K.D. Singh Babu thus silenced all his critics who had opined that he does not play in the interest of the team. He outshone all his teammates and bewildered the opponents. At the end of the match, the British captain said, 'These Indians are just world beaters but I did not think that they were going to have such a victory on a ground so unsuitable to their play. But tonight they showed how magnificent they are under any conditions.'

During the finals against England, the chairman of Holland's Hockey Federation was sitting next to Dr A.C. Chaterjee, team India manager, in the jury. He averred that India were lucky to win against Holland in the semi-final. Dr Chaterjee suggested to his counterpart, 'Let Holland play one more match against us.' The latter conceded and invited the Indian team to Amsterdam. Recalling this incidence in a tribute paid to K.D. Singh Babu in the *K.D. Singh Babu Memorial Society* magazine, Dr Chaterjee wrote:

'India again beat Holland by 5–1. Out of these, 3 were scored by the centre-forward and left-in through beautiful passes by Babu, and Babu himself scored 2. Thus, all the five goals had his stamp.'

The biggest upset of the Olympics was the struggle for third place between Pakistan and Holland. The first match was a 0–0 draw but in the replay, Holland beat Pakistan 4–1 and took the bronze. While India glorified itself with the gold, Pakistan's hunt for a place on the stands remained unfulfilled. The gold for India came just at the right moment; two days before it was to celebrate its second Independence Day. In one of his articles, K.D. Singh Babu wrote: 'The biggest moment of my life was when I heard the final whistle in the finals against England.' And truly, the euphoria was not just to do with the fact that India had won the gold but about how the whistle signalled his supremacy as the brains of the attack, the chief instigator, a player who constantly heeded the shouts, 'Babu, Babu, come on Babu' by the enthusiastic Indian supporters. Indeed, he was the main architect of an Indian victory. On his way back home, he brought two prized possessions, a .22 BSA sports rifle and a Raliegh sports bicycle. No sooner was he back on the streets of Barabanki, than this Olympic stalwart could be seen on the move on a sports cycle with a hockey stick to reach playing grounds.

The gold at the London Olympics had a special significance for K.D. Singh Babu. Not only was it the first gold for an independent India, it also brought back memories of his first meeting with Pandit Jawahar Lal Nehru at Barabanki before Independence. In an article written for *Swatantra Bharat* way back in 1964, he recalled that day when Pandit Nehru visited our ancestral house in Barabanki before independence. His eldest brother, Kr Rajendra Singh, was a freedom fighter and the family took the lead in the non-cooperation movement in the district. As a symbol of this movement, the family made a bonfire of English clothes in the presence of Pandit Nehru and young K.D. Singh Babu was introduced to him as a hockey player of great promise. Soon after, when the Indian hockey team landed in New Delhi in 1948, Prime Minister Nehru graced the occasion to watch an exhibition match and met members of the victorious team. Memories of the bonfire were still fresh in his mind and recognising K.D. Singh Babu, he patted him on the back. India had defeated England in the finals and Babu had played the major role. Pandit Nehru had the greatest satisfaction as authentic Indian fabric had scored over British tweed.

March towards Stardom 1949–1953

India has only a fifty-fifty chance but all depends on this Houdini of Indian hockey.

—Rex Rodrigues, member of the 1948 Indian Olympic team, about the credibility of K.D. Singh Babu before Helsinki Olympics, 1952; The Times of India, 1952

While concluding his report for the *Hindustan Times*, after the convincing and well won finals against England at the 1948 London Olympics, Berry Sarbhadikary wrote:

> *And so, once again, we are on the top of world hockey. But I wonder for how long. European hockey has been improving perceptibly so fast, as Pakistan's defeat would indicate. We would do well to pay heed to Dhyan Chand's warning [of] a few years ago and make efforts to improve our hockey, which, in patches, still amazes the hockey world.*
>
> *The gold medals have, after all, come to India. These were well deserved, but our exhibition of hockey, although the finest on this visit, would not compare favourably with that in the days of the wizards: Dhyan Chand, Roop Singh, Lal Shah or Jaffer.*

Although all the sports critics were full of praise for the game and the maturity displayed by K.D. Singh Babu, calling him the brains of the attack and the chief instigator, they were apprehensive about the improving standard of the game by European nations. Pakistan, which played the same style of hockey as Indians, was another source of danger from the sub-continent. While comparing the standard of Indian hockey witnessed during the 1948 Olympics with the Dhyan Chand era of 1928 to 1936, no one of them could visualise that during the days of Dhyan Chand, the opposing teams were very weak whereas in the twelve years that followed, the Europeans had worked hard and though their attack was not very cohesive or well-planned in comparison to the teams from the Indian sub-continent, they did offer a very stiff, packed defense. An added disadvantage was the heavy soft turf which did not suit the style of play of the Indians. Berry Sarbhadhikary had rightly pointed out that the defeat of Pakistan at the hands of England and Holland showed how well the European teams had learned the game. The Pakistan team had a lot of top players from undivided India and prominent among them were A.I.S. Dara who had played earlier with Dhyan Chand, Shahrukh, and others. These Pakistan stars were earlier members of a very formidable Punjab team and they had everything in them to come on top. As a matter of fact, it was expected that they might spring a surprise but if they could not do it, this was basically because they did not have a playmaker like K.D. Singh Babu in their team who bewildered every defense through all the matches that India played. Most of the time, Pinto, the Indian goalkeeper, had a relaxed time and often enough, he was seen resting against the pole nonchalantly. Adding to the pressure was the distribution of a pamphlet in all corners of London stating that England was going to win the Olympic gold based on their fine showing at the previous London Olympics. Whether the England team was full of confidence or they wanted to create a demoralising effect is not known, but their storming into the finals certainly gave an impression that the British team had prepared well.

The 1948 Olympics was a debut for all the players. In the pre-Olympic preparations back home in India and as has been described in the preceding chapter, K.D. Singh Babu had shown the selectors and hockey lovers his magical prowess. And he just showcased that at the London Olympics. That the first post-independence Olympic gold is largely credited to him is well documented in press reportage and was later on substantiated by Dr A.C. Chaterjee himself, in conversation with a *Hindustan Weekly* correspondent in an article that was published on Sunday, 28 August 1949. In the words of the team manager who was also the IHF secretary at that time:

> *Babu was always the chief brain behind our attacks and he was the one to get the greatest applause from the crowd in England as well as all over the continent. The most familiar and prominent shout from the crowd during our Olympic fixtures used to be, "Come along Babu" and Babu always responded and delighted the people with his masterly game—speed and ball control of the finest order.*

K.D. Singh Babu was always his brilliant self. He never had a lean patch, except on three occasions when he was not well. Representing United Provinces right from 1940, he was always the star forward. Even before his magnificent showing under the captainship of Dhyan Chand on the East Africa tour of 1947–48, the spotlight had turned to him. In the 1946 National Championship, UP were pitted against a strong Punjab side which included star players like A.I.S. Dara, Shahrukh, Balbir Singh, Amir Kumar, Aziz,Trilochan Singh, VedPrakash, and others. Though UP had a weak side, they gave a tough fight. The correspondent of *Illustrated Weekly* reported:

> *No praise is too high for the gallant and determined fight [put] up by United Provinces, who made their first appearance in the competition. Their forwards lacked the understanding and cohesion of their opponents, but, nevertheless, were full of ideas, particularly inside-right, Babu. He justified the reputation he has earned in the North of being one of the most dangerous dribblers in the game and the manner in which he utilised the through passes would have achieved better results but for the watchfulness of the Punjab defenders.*

In every match of his life he was the most marked man. Many a times, he was pushed around or surrounded by four to five opponents whose main aim was to see that he did not receive the ball. Quite often, such tactics failed. A UP vs. Patiala match is one such incident. A report in *The Statesman*, dated 4 March 1949 came out as follows:

> *In the National Hockey Championship played at Lady Hardinge ground, New Delhi, UP beat Patiala by 2 goals to nil. UP owed their success to their inside-right, Babu, who scored both the goals.*
>
> *Led by K.D. Singh, better known as Babu, who vice-captained the all-India team at the last Olympics at London, UP had things their own way for most of the game, Babu himself being responsible for opening and completing the tally.*
>
> *UP took the offensive right from bully off, and Patiala's only means of preventing them from taking an early lead was by marking Babu, playing inside-right. This they successfully did most of the time but could not completely hold the nimble-footed Babu, who, when he did get the possession of the ball, delighted the crowd with his fine stick work.*
>
> *Fortunately, Patiala had a good defense and never failed to clear hard when the UP forwards were crowding their goalmouth. UP should have taken advantage of Patiala's defenders marking Babu and should have fed their wingers more often.*

As Babu scored the first goal, stung by this reverse, Patiala retaliated strongly. So eager were Patiala to get an equaliser that they temporarily forgot Babu's presence on the field to their own misfortune for four minutes from the end, [and] an unmarked Babu pounced on a good centre from winger Prem and left the Patiala custodian no chance from close in.

Just before the scheduled Helsinki Olympics of 1952, the IHF were preparing to send another team to Kenya on a goodwill visit. Keeping in mind that the Helsinki Olympics were approaching, the IHF were fully convinced that given the reputation that he had earned as a schemer and a match winner, K.D. Singh Babu was the right choice to lead any Indian team. The Indian supremacy in world hockey could not be compromised, so he was the natural choice. His name was announced as the captain of the Kenya-bound team by the selection committee which comprised of P. Gupta (Chairman), R.D. Bhalla, Secretary, M.J. Vakil (Bombay) and C.R. Reddi (Madras).

The team consisted of:

Goalkeepers: K. Dessa Mutthu (Mysore) and Sardar Meher Singh (Patiala)

Backs: Wahiuddin (Railways), R.S. Gentle (Bombay), D. Pal (West Bengal)

Halves: Leslie Claudius (West Bengal), G. Pereira (Bombay), Hussain Ali (UP), Perumal (Bombay)

Forwards: C.S. Dubey (West Bengal), K.D. Singh Babu (UP), Jagdish Singh (Delhi), Hardial Singh (Services), Gurbachan Singh (Delhi), Rajgopal (Mysore), Siva Prakashan (Madras)

Also included as standbys were Mohanlal (Maharashtra), Swaroop Singh (Faridkot), Trilok Singh (Delhi), Pillay (Maharasthra) and L. Fernandes (Bombay)

After the team and its captain were announced, Ashwini Kumar of Punjab Hockey Association charged the selection committee with communalism. He was apparently unhappy about the exclusion of one of his blue-eyed boys from the team who he wished would lead the team; it was a primary effort on his part to put his favourite player firmly in saddle to lead the future Indian hockey team to the Helsinki Olympics. Replying to his charges and speaking to the press, Dr A.C. Chaterjee said:

As far as I can understand, Mr Kumar misunderstood the communication from the Ministry of Education advising the IHF to include in their Kenya

> *team as far as possible representatives of all interests. So far, no one of the states affiliated to IHF have accused it for selection on communal lines. We have been, many a time, criticised for some omissions and commissions in our selection of Olympic teams, but even these critics never blamed us for selecting teams on communal lines. Mr Ashwini Kumar should have come out with his objection in the very beginning when it was announced by the IHF that it had authorised Mr Naval Tata, its president, to select the team's captain for Kenya. Naval Tata was a great admirer of K.D. Singh Babu and for him, truly and justifiably, there could be no one else but him.*

So it was more than apparent that the main objection raised by Ashwini Kumar was the announcement of K.D. Singh Babu as captain of the team. It is not recorded anywhere as to who it was that Ashwini Kumar was lobbying for, but one thing became very clear—right from 1951, politics and partiality in sports had started taking roots. Dhyan Chand and Berry Sarbhadhikary had cautioned about such eventualities. And happen it did. Players started associating with different godfathers, throwing the larger interest of the nation to the winds.

In his career, K.D. Singh Babu not only had to tackle the players of the opposing teams, but most of the time, he also found no good support from his teammates. Adding to his problem were the over-enthusiastic press. Even though before the 1948 Olympics, they had started to compare him with the legendary Dhyan Chand, at times they called his game 'selfish' without understanding the reason why he held on to the ball for long periods. And now, the fourth factor had come into play, the likes of Ashwini Kumars who would one day control the IHF. It is remarkable that despite all sorts of handicaps, he continued to swim against the current and make big headlines. As Bobby Talyarkhan had written, it was true that a lot of people felt jealous of him and some of them made every possible effort to jeopardise his career, whereas he was the one who created players who would otherwise have been relegated to oblivion.

A couple of days before the IHF team was about to leave for Kenya, they played an exhibition match against a combined Railways at Cooperage which they won, 4–0. Apart from what the press wrote about the game, its main feature was again a commentary on the display of K.D. Singh Babu which read as follows:

> *Skipper Babu was his usual brilliant self; his clever positioning that always found him unmarked, his sure trapping of the most ferocious Gentle drives, and his defense-splitting through passes that invariably caught his opponents flat-footedwere a real treat to watch.*

During the East Africa tour of 1951, the all-India team played a total of 35 matches, and won all by huge margins. The *Mombassa Times* in one of its reports said that goals came by the baker's dozen. Out of a total of 236 goals scored by the India team, K.D. Singh Babu alone scored 93. Though it is not necessary here to go into the details of the matches, these being of no significance, the correspondents of *The Goan Voice* and *Bombay Chronicle* who had accompanied the team wrote gloriously about the mastery of K.D. Singh Babu. Watching him play against Kenya Eleven, one press report said:

> *All-India's attack has come to depend entirely on Babu, and the captain has accepted this heavy responsibility remarkably well.*

This is exactly what was being said and written during the exhibition matches played just before the London Olympics.

In the match against a hurriedly assembled Tanga team, which the all-India team won, 12–1, K.D. Singh Babu scored 7 goals and delighted the crowd by adopting newer methods of scoring. In one such goal, he flicked the ball over the heads of the crowd in the striking circle which also included a burly goalkeeper, MacEwan, of European descent, and his final goal came as a cricket shot into the back of the net.

After the match against Nairobi, which all-India trounced, 11–0, the press wrote:

> *Digvijai Singh Babu was the man of the match. At his brilliant best, his superb stick work had returned to him completely, bringing back memories of the 1947 tour. Switching to centre-forward, he scored five goals and had a hand in most of the others. He was the inspiration and leader of the whole line. His last and the team's eleventh goal was the best goal seen in Nairobi. He cut through three defenders, dribbled round the goalie almost to the post, and calmly placed the ball through a space of three inches—an individual effort that brought the crowd to its feet.*

On the tour, Kisumu Eleven got the worst treatment as they lost by a mind-boggling score of 17–0.

Back home after a successful tour of East Africa, preparations started for the forthcoming Helsinki Olympics of 1952. During the early stages, nothing much could be said about the composition of the team and the most important factor was as to who would lead the team. India still reigned supreme in world hockey and though one critic who was a member of the 1948 playing squad gave only a fifty-fifty chance to India, others did believe that with K.D. Singh Babu spearheading the attack, India was sure to come out in flying colors again. Though K.D. Singh Babu himself was quite sure of being appointed captain, he had no idea that danger to his career had resurfaced. Politics of favouritism had quietly slipped into the selection committee room. After his suspension way back in 1946 and some opposition for his captaincy on the recent East Africa tour, this was the third time in his career that he was being pushed around. Trials and exhibition matches started and critics were back on the job. Yet in the nationals and exhibition matches, he continued to outshine all.

Meanwhile, news had trickled in about the rankings of various teams by the IHF at the Helsinki Olympics. The Indian selectors and the various organisations as well as some aspirants for captaincy of the Indian team were quite aware of the growing prowess of England and Holland and adding to their discomfort was the placement of Pakistan as the team ranked number two, after India. If India had a chance to retain hockey supremacy, it was only possible while K.D. Singh Babu was around. So who would not have thought of leading the team when India was sure to win? Manipulations started within the selection committee and the name of Balbir Singh Sr was being pushed forward to captain the side.

Though in the nationals held in Calcutta on 15 March 1952, UP were eliminated by Bengal by a solitary goal in the quarter-finals, it was again K.D. Singh Babu who stole the limelight. Three different newspapers gave a scintillating account of his masterly display and singled him out by splashing varied decorative headlines highlighting his wizardry.

UP Beaten But Not Disgraced: Superb Display by Babu

A spectacularly flashy movement between Gurung and Dubey surprised an otherwise stolid UP defense and brought about the match winner for Bengal in the fifth minute after [the] interval, but apart from this goal and the victory, Bengal had hardly much to enthuse over their display.

UP, on the other hand, played pleasing and inspiring hockey, thanks mainly to their Olympic inside-right Babu whose splendid stick work and unstoppable scheming marked him out as the best player of the country at the moment.

Here was indeed a glorious remembrance of what the game once was in India and never since the retirement of that all-time great "hockey wizard"—the great Dhyan Chand—had people been treated to such amazing jugglery with the stick and serpentine movement with the ball.

> *This one Babu, in the UP attack whenever he was in possession of the ball, seemed to have shaken the Bengal defense to its very foundation and if the home goal survived a fall, that was partly due to good luck and partly due to the sterling performance of their two wing half-backs, Da Luz and Claudius. Facing Babu, Da Luz had a difficult task ahead but he played his best game of the season and when he was a little tired in the closing minutes, Claudius rose to rare heights by saving at least three positive goals.*
>
> *Even in the first half, when Bengal had the territorial advantage, the UP raids looked more penetrating. Babu was a class by himself and if only the centre-forward and the right-winger beside him had shown better judgement and sense of anticipation, he might have brought devastation to the home side.*

A news item appearing in *Anand Bazar Patrika* described his game as follows:

> **Luck Deserts UP in National Hockey: Babu's Wizardry**
>
> *Although Bengal won through Gurung's clever opportunism, the match left the impression that UP were definitely unlucky to have lost. UP not only played cleverer hockey, but also had definitely better scoring chances. But cruel Lady Luck would never smile on them. Truth to tell, it was UP's match but Bengal made a bargain of it.*
>
> *But whereas everybody in [the] UP team played cleverly, Abid Ali, Malhotra and Babu, their skipper inside-right, outshone the rest. Babu had a stamp of genius which made him the star forward on the field. He gave an exceptionally brilliant display which should easily earn him a place in India's team for [the] Helsinki Games. But Babu's colleagues failed to keep pace with him, otherwise UP would have equalised or clinched a victory. Babu was tricky like an "eel" who would always wriggle his way through a bunch of rival defenders. Above all was his deliciously clean hockey which was highly appreciated.*

K.D. Singh Babu was well aware of the campaign in favour of Balbir Singh by some members of Punjab Hockey Association who had built a strong clout in hockey circles, yet he remained undisturbed and showed his class and mastery in the nationals. While the press painted a glorious picture of his game which was enough to shatter anyone's claim for captaincy, some members of the selection committee tried their best to pull the rug from under his feet. Finally, it was the decisive vote of the chairman of the committee, Dr A.C. Chaterjee, which decided the matter in his favour and on 18 March 1952 his name was announced as the captain of the Helsinki-bound team. Thus, the third hurdle too was crossed.

Bengal went on to become the national champions in 1952. Thereafter followed an exhibition match between champions Bengal and Rest on 22 March 1952. The two teams were constituted as follows:

Bengal:
Mendies, R. Das, D. Pal, Leslie Claudius, Jaswant Raput and Da Luz, Dubey, Gurung and Carapiet, Jansen and Harjinder Singh

The Rest:
Francis (Madras), Swarup Singh (Services), R.S. Gentle (Bombay), Malhotra (UP), Bakshi (Services), Perumal (Bombay), Kishen Lal (Railways; Captain 1948 Olympics), K.D. Singh Babu (UP), Balbir Singh (Punjab), Udham Singh (Punjab), and Sethi (Services)

While in this match, the Rest defeated the champions, Bengal, by a solitary goal, once more it was K.D. Singh Babu who caught the most attention and the press again wrote a glorious account:

Outstanding in the winner's forward line was inside-right Babu, who touched peak form in the second half. Controlling the ball with deft twists of the wrist and applying the right amount of body swerve with every move, he bamboozled man after man, making some of them look silly.

Babu was ably assisted by Kishen Lal on the right with whom he established a perfect understanding. But whereas the Rest's right flank was in good working order, the left was badly out of touch and Balbir in the middle was a little too lackadaisical.

Another report said:

The Rest of India defeated the new champions, Bengal, by a solitary goal in an exhibition match played here today. The Rest were the superior combination and dominated the exchanges. It was only good goalkeeping by Mendies that enabled Bengal to leave the field narrowly beaten.

The Rest forwards pinned Bengal in their own area and the mastery of Babu was evident. Babu played a great game and is sure to be the favourite abroad with his dazzling stick work. Against an experienced half-line, he tore through them at will and only Mendies in the goal could stop him.

By outshining every other player in this exhibition match, he had again justified the confidence of Dr Chaterjee as he had done earlier during the London Olympics held in 1948. As it turned out, the press and hockey fans saw that Balbir Singh Sr was no match for his artistry and that he earned the crown of captaincy solely on the basis of his magic spell.

The same day names of twenty-seven probables were announced for the Helsinki Olympics. They were as under:

Goalkeepers:
Francis (Madras), Deshmuthu (Mysore) and Mendies (Bengal)

Backs:
Swaroop Singh (Services), R.S. Gentle (Bombay), Dharam Singh (Punjab), Wahidulla (Railways), D. Pal (Bengal), and Balkrishna Singh (Pepsu)

Halves:
Leslie Claudius (Bengal), Keshav Dutta (Bengal), Da Luz (Bengal), Jaswant Rajput (Bengal), Malhotra (UP), Perumal (Bombay), Bhaskaran (Mysore) and Bakshish Singh (Services)

Forwards:
KishenLal (Railways), K.D. Singh Babu (UP), Balbir Singh (Punjab), Udham Singh (Punjab), Rajgopal (Mysore), Raghbir Lal (Punjab), C.S. Dubey (Bengal), C.S. Gurung (Bengal), G. Singh (Services), and S.D. Sethi (Services)

As trials and training was to start in May, beginning from Calcutta and then on to Dehradun, the twenty-seven probables were subject to the watchful eyes of the coaches, N.N. Mukerjee and Harbail Singh as also the selection committee. Only seventeen or eighteen were set to make it to Helsinki. Before the players could be subjected to the rigours of this process, Reginald Rodrigues, who was a member of the 1948 Olympic team but was indisposed to participate, aired his view about the chances of this team in an article carried by *The Times of India* on 30 March 1952. A summary of his viewpoint is reproduced below:

INDIA HAS ONLY A FIFTY-FIFTY CHANCE OF RETAINING TITLE

Old Brigade, The Backbone of Olympic Hockey Team —Reg Rodrigues

It is the easiest thing in the world to fall from a pinnacle, and unlike our cricket cavaliers who will soon sally forth to England's green swards with nothing to lose and everything to gain, our hockey hopes will take wing in June to defend the one and only good mark to India's credit in the stern arena of international sport.

The years past have seen this country sitting on velvet so far as the Olympic hockey title was concerned, but the days when our teams went across as masters to backwards students are definitely over.

While I do not subscribe to the views of the old timers who secretly believe that they could step on the field and make circles around the new generations of stick-wielders without any more training than a haircut and a shave, I do believe that our chances of retaining the title at Helsinki this year are now a fifty-fifty proposition when compared with the taken-for-granted position of the days of yore.

Right now [it] is the calm before the storm of selection breaks. From the middle of May, twenty-seven of India's hopefuls start a period of training and trial at Calcutta, with eighteen to make the final trek along the Olympic highway. Fame or failure? To me the answer lies in the critical period of selection, for I have always maintained that our greatest danger to the retention of the Olympic title comes from within and not without. Provincialism, favouritism and egotism, time and again, have raised their ugly head, and only the very naïve can believe otherwise in this headlong rush for the coveted ticket to Helsinki.

Old Brigade

On form, India's team to Helsinki presents no problem to me. Dependence on the old Olympic brigade is emphasised in the selector's inclusion of Bengal's Keshav Dutt and Bombay's Kishen Lal among the trainees. Dutt has not figured in the national championship for the last two years but if this polished half-back can touch even half the form he showed four years back, he is still streets ahead of any pivot in the country today.

Kishen Lal has been seen more in the inside than the outside berth since he returned with his triumphant 1948 side, but again, he is far and away the cleverest wingman among the poorest crop of 'flyers' India has had for many a year. *What is more important still is that this former Olympic captain goes with inside-right Babu like a smoker's cigarette goes with its early morning cup of coffee.*

> **Houdini[1] of Indian Hockey**
>
> *Uttar Pradesh's Babu has been honoured with the captaincy of the Helsinki side and while I doubt his suitability for this responsible role off the field, the genius of this Houdini of Indian Hockey who can escape the tightest ring of defenders with the ridiculous ease of a true artist cannot be denied.*

Peering deeper into my old crystal ball, I see to the left of Kishen and Babu in the forward line-up, Punjab's Balbir Singh, Udham Singh and Raghbir Lal. The utter dearth of centre-forwards in this country today makes Balbir an automatic choice, though his marksmanship will have to be a 100 per cent improvement on his Wembley performance way back in 1948. Udham Singh and the young, fast and versatile Raghbir Lal should work India's left flank, though I am convinced the inside-left's style of play will not be such a success under foreign conditions. Oh for a Jansen here, instead.

Backbone of the Team

The backbone of any team, anywhere, anytime is the half-line, and India is fortunate in still having a classy bunch in this department, though the last Wembley line-up of Keshav Dutt, Amir Kumar and MaElevene Vaz will take a lot of beating. If it is presumed that Keshav Dutt is being groomed for the pivotal birth—and that is obvious—then Bengal's Leslie Claudius is undoubtedly the player for the right-half position. Bombay's Perumal who missed his Olympic colours by a whisker in 1948 should be right there at left-half if fate doesn't go back on him again.

The magnificent form of the Services' Swarup Singh in the national championship this year makes him an outstanding choice for the right-back post and it is here that India is stronger than she was in London where Punjab's Trilochan Singh proved a failure. A suitable partner for Swarup

[1] Harry Houdini was an Austro-Hungarian born American stage magician noted for his sensational escape acts.

Singh would be either Bombay's Gentle or Punjab's Dharam Singh. This is, to my mind, the only close tussle for a position.

Last, and by no means the least, is the vital final line of defense. Here there should be no hesitation in nominating Francis of Madras. A cut above the other goalkeepers, with Mysore's flamboyant Deshmuthu included, Francis is the only player who can fill the boots and pads of the great Leo Pinto.

Rodrigues concluded:

So far so good. We have the goods to put it across to the world, but good captaincy and managership are also an essential part of the fight for world honours. The London trip was marred with such unpleasantries in this connection and could have proved disastrous. I feel that the Helsinki adventure may head the same way if [the] bombastic managers do not get off their high horse in time and realise that, after all, they are but servants of the team. If all this goes well, India can keep her hockey reputation untarnished inspite of Pakistan's psychological edge on us, Holland's growing reputation, Great Britain's never-say-die spirit and Japan's habit of pulling a rabbit out of the bag.

All said and done, we have the necessary ingredients to keep us sitting pretty on top of the hockey world. Let us not sit there in smug complacency. The retention of the title lies not in adapting ourselves to the Western technique but in getting down to business with a will, free of prejudice, free of pettiness and free of impartiality. And then, maybe, I shall not have to say *I told you so*.

Rodrigues' surgical analysis clearly pointed to two main factors. First, that by 1948, England, Holland and Pakistan had markedly emerged as a force in hockey that threatened the supremacy of India in future and coupled with this was the backroom manipulation in selecting the best formation to represent India. Politics to dominate the Federation had already taken a firm seat way back in 1951 and with the departure of Dhyan Chand from international participation, the field was open to project favourite protégés to lead the side. When Rodrigues wrote about preconceived ideas in selecting the team, he indirectly hinted that prejudices and partiality would one day harm the interest of the nation so far as hockey was concerned. And he was not wrong. There was an attempt to sabotage the credibility of K.D. Singh Babu to lead the team despite the fact that in years gone by, he had emerged as the top player of the country whom Rodrigues had appropriately called as 'The Houdini of Indian Hockey' and the only one with undisputed ability to pierce any defense. At that time, it was widely accepted that if India were to retain the gold at the Helsinki Olympics, all depended on one man—K.D. Singh Babu, yet attempts were made to steal the thunder from him. He was a one-man army around whom the rest of the players revolved like planets around the sun. That this was true became clear during the Olympic events of 1952 and thereafter.

The team for Helsinki was finally announced in June 1952 and the most noticeable omission was that of the former captain of the 1948 team, Kishen Lal, who was replaced by C.S. Dubey of Bengal, often referred to as 'Speedy Dubey'. The team constitution was well-balanced and read as follows:

K.D. Singh Babu, Captain (UP), R. Francis (Madras), C. Desmuthu (Mysore), R.S. Gentle (Bomaby), Dharam Singh (Punjab), Swarup Singh (Services), L. Claudius (Bengal), Keshav Dutt (Bengal), G. Perumal (Bombay), Jaswant Singh (Bengal), Raghbir Lal (Punjab), C.S. Dubey (Bengal), Balbir Singh (Punjab), Grahnandan Singh (Services), Udham Singh (Punjab), M. Rajgopal (Mysore), M. Da Luz (Bengal) and C.S. Gurung (Bengal)

For the choice of vice-captain, there were two contenders. K.D. Singh Babu favoured Keshav Dutt while the top cops of Punjab Hockey Association were supporting the name of Balbir Singh. Raghbir Lal recalls that during the voting by team members, when he cast his vote in favour of Keshav Dutt, he was hauled up by the top brass of the Punjab police for disobeying their orders. A whip was issued for Balbir Singh and some players, believing that some of these officers were on the ascendency to occupy the top slot in IHF in years to come, voted for Balbir Singh to save their future interest. The die had been cast and the future of Indian hockey was gradually slipping into the pockets of uniformed civil services men.

Before leaving Calcutta for Copenhagen, K.D. Singh Babu said, 'My team is as strong as the one we sent in 1948. I do not believe in forecasting the future and only our performance will show where we stand. Though we have got very little encouragement from our countrymen, we will try our utmost to bring glory to India.'

He made this statement because of the internal squabbles within the IHF which nearly sabotaged his captaincy and also because of comments by some critics who had been painting a bad scenario even before the team left the shores. He had a tough job on hand but at the back of his mind was the confidence that Dr Chaterjee had shown in him. It is startling that while on one hand, the IHF had no money to cover the travel expenses of the team to Helsinki, on the other, when it came to selections, they showed their authority. To cover the expenses, the team played an exhibition match in Jamshedpur against Jamshedpur Eleven where a huge crowd assembled to watch the national team. The Olympians beat the Jamshedpur Eleven by a huge margin of nine to nil and to show that he was the right choice for captain, K.D. Singh Babu scored four, and with this confidence, he led the team to Helsinki.

Dr A.C. Chaterjee, the 1948 Olympic team manager who had vast experience of European hockey, said that the Indian team, as it stood after the period of training, was at least three goals better than any other team in the world. However, the press again commented that unlike in previous years, this skipper's job in Finland will be no sinecure.

HELSINKI 1952

Before the Indian team was chosen, there were adverse comments in many directions to the effect that the standard of hockey at the moment in India was low and that the team of 1952 was the weakest that India had ever sent out in quest of Olympic honours. And then doubts were being raised about the capabilities of a new captain and a new manager to maintain India's position and status. Burdened with such criticism, the Indian hockey team finally reached Helsinki after acclimatising at Copenhagen. Helsinki had been experiencing wet weather and a very cold wind had been blowing. The Indian camp sent up special prayers to the weather gods.

Though they beat Austria, 4–0, in the quarter-finals their performance did not satisfy the critics. In the semi-finals against England, the Indian team had a tough time. As reported, the Indian forward line was very disjointed and the defense carried the entire burden. However, India beat England convincingly, 3–1, to enter the finals.

In the other group, Holland had trounced Pakistan by a solitary goal to meet India in the finals. On the day of the final, that is 24 August, the weather kept fine and though early in the day, there were clouds hovering in the sky, the ground was in top order, although it was on the slower side. As events unfolded, the Indian team, inspired by K.D. Singh Babu, played their best match of the Olympics. The whole team moved like a well-oiled machine and every team member gave his best. One critic wrote, 'Viewing the match as a whole, my impression was that Keshav Dutt, Claudius and Gentle were outstanding in India's defense while Raghbir Lal, Babu and

Balbir Singh shone in the attack.' Commenting further, he added, 'Babu, India's captain, produced his usual form in the final. He toyed with the opposition but was not selfish. India's centre-forward Balbir Singh had another great personal triumph.'

The match analysis clearly showed that while sharpshooter Balbir Singh was very effective inside the striking circle in the 6–1 win, three of his five goals came from excellent passes by K.D. Singh Babu who put the opposition on the wrong foot and gave open chances to Balbir Singh who did not miss the mark. Babu himself scored one and it was said that he and Balbir Singh missed many chances. By half-time, India were leading, 4–0. After resumption of play, the score read 5–0. Then the Indian goalkeeper made a mistake. Feeling exuberant that India were already leading by 5–0, he took the liberty to clear a ball by rushing up to the touch line and Holland's inside-left R.T. Esser made no mistake in scoring. In the thirtieth minute, India forced a short corner which was again converted by Balbir Singh.

In the second half, India forced a few more short corners but the Dutch goalkeeper, Mulder, made nice saves. Towards the end, India slackened. They could have scored more goals with some luck, but they appeared to be content with the margin of goals already achieved.

This spectacular convincing win had silenced all the critics back home and India had retained her supremacy in the world of hockey. What was injudiciously said to be the weakest India team that ever participated in the Olympics turned the tables. The PTI correspondent who was covering the match wrote:

> *India won the Olympic Hockey Championship today and thus retained the world title which has been theirs since the last quarter of a century. At the Velodrome, special Olympic hockey ground, they decisively beat Holland by 6 goals to 1.*
>
> *The Indian forward line today moved in accordance with a carefully prepared plan which was brilliantly executed by skipper Babu and centre-forward Balbir Singh.*

Though Balbir Singh netted five goals, the press singled out the goal scored by K.D. Singh Babu as the best of the match when it wrote:

> *After being completely outclassed in the first half when their robust tactics paid no dividends, the Dutch in the second half decided to meet polish with polish, science with science. This change in their mode immediately paid*

> *rich dividends in the form of their only goal of the match scored by R.T. Esser, their inside-left whose successful shot was as spectacular as that of Babu in the first half.*

When the final whistle went up, 5000 thrilled spectators rose to give India a hearty cheer for their undisputed supremacy in hockey. Rein De Waal, manager of the Dutch team said, 'It was a great game. The Indians were very fast and on the run of play they ought to have won. I knew they were very good but I did not know they were so good to beat Holland by 6–1. Our defense was a bit weak before India's forward line. It was a great pity that the ground was dry which the Indians love.'

The British Manager, R. Ynfison, said, 'There is no doubt that India showed their supremacy in the game this afternoon. They were complete masters in all departments of the game.'

As the medals were being given, three beautiful Finnish girls in their native costumes advanced with bouquets of carnations and presented them to all the members of the three teams. India's captain, K.D. Singh Babu, acknowledged the flowers by kissing the girls' hands. Commenting on the performance of his team, K.D. Singh Babu said, 'We are happy we have once again retained the championship and I am sure people in India will welcome the news. My colleagues were not only excellent hockey players but they played as a team, everyone co-operating with everyone else to the fullest extent.'

The victory at the Olympics was followed by exhibition matches in Germany, Holland and England. The Indian team again played against Germany, Holland and the All Europe team. They beat All Europe, 5–1, and Holland again, 6–1. Speaking to the press, K.D. Singh Babu said, 'Thus we once more established our Olympic victory and impressed upon the world that our win over Holland in the Olympic finals was not a lucky affair.'

Then the team stopped in England for an exhibition match against Indian Gymkhana at Osterley which also included some English players who had participated at the Olympics. Confident as ever, K.D. Singh Babu showed his class with a display that left spectators totally bewildered. A London correspondent watching the game put it this way:

Babu's Masterly Display

> *India's victorious hockey team gave an exhibition of the game well worthy of the world champions that they are against a not untalented side at the*

Indian Gymkhana Club at Osterley, near London, at the conclusion of their European tour.

Their forwards were swift and incisive, their half-line alert and thrustful, their backs bold and reliant. Consequently, their Madras goalkeeper, Francis, had little to do and he dealt confidently with one or two clearances he had to make.

In a star-studded side, it was Babu the skipper who outshone all others while playing inside-right. Babu used the stick with great delicacy. Sometimes, he used it with the proficiency of a billiard player. At other times, it was a rapier in his hands for a lightning thrust of the ball past a bewildered opponent. Next, it became a spoon with which to scoop the ball over the heads of on-rushing defenders to feed his waiting wingers. Yet other times, he would weave his way through a wall of defenders and in so doing, give the impression that the ball was attached to his stick by means of an elastic thread. Then, finally, his stick became a sword with which to slash the ball into the goal.

When the Gymkhana's side broke into Indian territory, the champions' defense would close in to padlock their goalmouth. Except for R.A. Norris, Great Britain's centre-forward who played as inside-right for Gymkhana, the home side was composed of players born and bred in India and well acquainted with the highest standards of the game there. Yet, try as they did, they were unable to reply even once to India's eight goals. A stronger side might have prevented the Indian team from indulging in as many individual efforts as marked the game. But despite this, few passes went astray and the cohesion and understanding between the players was exemplary.

The write-up concluded:

The team's unblemished record of successes, both in Helsinki and elsewhere in Europe, guarantees the preservation of India's repeatedly demonstrated hockey supremacy in the future. K.D. Singh Babu has successfully demolished all ill thoughts about what was being said earlier and [proved] that he was destined to be acclaimed as the best hockey player of the world. It was a unique performance under all pressures. Somewhere in Pakistan, his coach, Mushfiq-ul-Zaman, must have rejoiced as well.

On 16 August, the team arrived at Calcutta. K.D. Singh Babu, the captain of the victorious hockey team, was the first to disembark and he was garlanded by Captain Rakshit on behalf of the governor of West Bengal as he stepped out of the Bharat Airways Skymaster. Naresh Kumar, India's number one tennis player, also arrived by the same flight. He had won the

Irish and Welsh championships and went up to the quarter-finals of the Wimbledon Plate. Sardar Harbail Singh, the coach of the Indian hockey team who arrived with the team, told the reporters, 'Babu's footwork and jugglery with the stick often dazed the foreigners. He was brilliantly assisted by Keshav Dutt, R.S. Gentle, Raghbir Lal and Balbir Singh. Our goalkeepers were never seriously tested.'

The Indian victory had finally sealed the mouths of those who used to criticise K.D. Singh Babu for being selfish on the field. The Houdini of Indian hockey had once again shown that with the co-operation of his teammates, he could weave a magic spell and it all depended on his teammates to exploit the openings that he created for them. He indeed proved to be a playmaker and that is exactly why Dr A.C. Chaterjee supported him for captaincy. What the critics had commented before the departure of the team for Finland, that this skipper's job will be no sinecure, had been proven to be damn true, and he did work very hard indeed to justify his captaincy with a masterly display. A team that left India relying on resources collected from an exhibition match amidst criticism and doubts about its performance and credibility arrived back triumphant to floral tributes and a dancing nation.

The team then reached New Delhi to play an exhibition match against a star-studded Delhi Hockey Association Eleven and as the two teams marched past to a pleasant tune, Prime Minister Jawaharlal Nehru took the salute. In the match, Udham Singh, playing in the inside-left position, showed what a great player he was by scoring two beautiful goals when the Olympic side beat DHA, 4–0. The press noted that he wove a few delicate patterns and for a moment, looked like he was eclipsing the other great artist, K.D. Singh Babu! It is unfortunate that in the years that followed, this great forward, Udham Singh, could not get the top job as such decisions of the IHF were influenced more by personal likes and dislikes rather than merit. However, at the Melbourne Olympics in 1956, it was he who led the team in absence of an injured Balbir Singh, and brought honours despite having being sidelined initially for the top job. Udham Singh was an energetic and class player who could fit in many positions and had misfortune not spoiled his chances before the 1948 Olympics because of an injury, he could have been the only one to represent India in five Olympics right from 1948 to 1964.

In the evening, the players from the two sides were entertained at a gala party at Chelmsford Club and among the dignitaries who graced the occasion were Sardar Swaran Singh and Rajkumari Amrit Kaur. Thereafter, K.D. Singh Babu and his close friend, R.S. Gentle, moved on to Barabanki where a civic reception awaited them which was graced by the governor of UP, His Excellency Shri K.M. Munshi. A little-known town, Barabanki, had overnight catapulted to national fame. K.D. Singh Babu was one among the family of hockey players destined to bring this glory back on the streets of Barabanki which used to be his practice surface during the formative days. What started as a solo effort on the streets of Barabanki way back in the early forties culminated in a march towards stardom on the victory fields of Helsinki.

Icing on the Cake: World Helms Award

Babu—Asia's Athlete of the Year.

—*Tribute to Indian Hockey. Six Top Athletes of the World Chosen. Los Angeles.*

The convincing 1952 Olympic victory marked him out as the most dangerous forward in the world. Earlier, even before the 1948 Olympics, he had been compared to Dhyan Chand and now, apart from being a master juggler, he had become a playmaker to reckon with. He could literally lay the plans after testing the strength and weakness of the opposing teams in the opening minutes of the game.

Then in 1953, recognising his capabilities as a champion artist, Mr N.N. Mitter, the Secretary of Bhowanipur Hockey Club, sent a request to him to play for the club in the Senior Hockey League Championship. He accepted the offer and joined the team as its captain.

Bhowanipur Club had a chequered history in local hockey. They first came to be associated with the senior league in 1932 and played for seven years. In 1939, they had the unenviable fate of being relegated into the second division. Then again in 1943, Bhowanipur earned their promotion to the senior division on the sheer merit and skill of their players and ever since then, they continued to play in the senior division without a break. In 1951, they were the joint leaders with Mohun Bagan but lost in the championship match by a solitary goal. And then in 1952, they were placed third in the league table. The club had a long cherished desire to be the league champions. And they wanted someone who could deliver. It was then that N.N. Mitter thought of asking K.D. Singh Babu to play for the club. The request was accepted and he was appointed captain of the team. It was a unique feature of Babu's character that he always led from the front and gave importance to the interest of the team. In the midst of the game, he would confer with his teammates and lay plans like an army general. And it was for these qualities apart from his personal abilities that he remained the undisputed top choice. Accepting the big responsibility thrust on him, he led Bhowanipur to glorious victory in the league championship. Next morning, *Anand Bazar Patrika* came out with a dazzling account of the game which read as follows:

> **Bhowanipur New Hockey Champions: Customs Taste Defeat in Concluding League Fixtures**
>
> *Speculations for the Senior Hockey League Championship of 1953 were set at rest on Saturday, when Bhowanipur, joint unbeaten leaders with Customs, met each other to try conclusions before the largest crowd so far on C.F.C. ground. The match, which was played as the third charity during the present hockey season, ended in a deserving victory for Bhowanipur by a solitary goal to nil. Ambition thus triumphed over tradition, especially as the customs has to its credit the hockey league champions honours on no fewer than a dozen occasions.*
>
> *Bhowanipur captain, Babu the skipper of the Olympic hockey team at the last Helsinki Olympic Games, must have brought with him the luck of Olympic hockey and infused it into this club. Babu was evidently the happiest man in the country for having pushed his new club to Olympic heights of glory. Babu had always been a never-failing source of inspiration to his teammates, who also showed excellent team spirit throughout the league. Shri N.N. Mitter, the live wire secretary of the club, has good reasons to feel elated because he was the man behind the screen to lead his team to such a glorious triumph.*
>
> *The Bhowanipur club tent was crowded during the evening and scenes of jubilation were witnessed inside the tent and in the club's enclosure. Everyone was eager to meet Babu, the captain of the league champions and Shri N.N. Mitter, their buoyant secretary, and convey their message of congratulations to them. There were fireworks on the ground for the entertainment of members and their friends.*
>
> *There was absolutely no fluke about Bhowanipur's victory on Saturday. Capably led by that master artist, Babu (K.D. Singh), India's Olympic skipper, Bhowanipur playing like a team inspired simply outplayed and outclassed the Customs for the greater proportion of the game, particularly in the first half. Babu delighted the crowd with an exhibition of hockey that will not easily be forgotten. With his clever dribbling and stick work, Babu was a constant menace to the opposing defense which could find no counter to his wiles.*

> *Babu provided the first thrill of the match when, in the third minute, he beat man after man and provided his centre-forward Kabir Ahmed with a lovely pass over which the centre-forward fumbled. Kabir Ahmed, who replaced Din Dayal, the leading goal scorer in the league, worked hard but he was responsible for throwing away several easy scoring opportunities.*
>
> *The Customs as a team played below expectations. Except for brief spells, their forwards were seldom in the picture. Ravi Deo, the pivot and L. Claudius, the right-half worked tirelessly throughout but they were busy defending their own citadel so much so that they were not of much assistance to their forwards. Their goalkeeper P. Cleur, however, brought some excellent saves, otherwise the victory margin would have been more than 1–0.*

Leading Bhowanipur to victory by clever planning, K.D. Singh Babu had again shown to the world what a fine repository he was of the core qualities needed to be the captain of a winning team. No one worth the name at that time had this unique quality of meticulous planning which he demonstrated so efficiently. He had again silenced his critics who had left no stone unturned in sabotaging his selection for captaincy of the Indian team to Helsinki. Covering the league matches for *Bombay Chronicle*, A.F.S. (Bobby) Talyarkhan, the most celebrated sports critic of that time, wrote:

> *Outstanding was K.D. Singh Babu whose stick work and ball control were really uncanny. Playing totally different hockey when he came for the Invitation Cup with Bhowanipur, the India Olympic captain of 1952 proved to be a wizard, both in distribution and individual attack. He made circles round the rather slow defenders and old Jameson had a broad smile on his face as he tried abortive conclusions to stop the weaving, winding Babu. If this is how he played at Helsinki, I can quite understand that what Gentle said over Radio Ceylon was dead true, that Babu was the maestro of Olympic hockey last year.*

THE ICING ON THE CAKE: HELMS WORLD TROPHY

The Helms Athletic Foundation, a sports organisation based in Los Angeles, California, USA, came into eElevenstence in 1936 with the express purpose to honour top sportspersons of the world in a somewhat similar way that Noble Foundation recognised achievements in scientific studies, literature and peace by individuals and organisations. The Helms World Trophy was given to one athlete from each of the six continents—Asia, Europe,

North America, South America, Africa and Australasia—for individual achievements.

With memories of the 1952 Helsinki Games still fresh in the minds of hockey enthusiasts, conversations in coffee shops and sports arenas continued to be largely analytically inclined, discussing as to who was the main hero of the 1952 Olympics triumph. Then one fine day in 1953 came the announcement from the Helms Hall Board. It had chosen the top six world athletes, one from each continent. And the name of K.D. Singh Babu figured as the top athlete of Asia for the 1952 Olympic Games. He was the first Indian to get this most coveted award. The Helms announcement finally settled the debate in coffee shops. Babu was now undisputedly the best hockey player of the world. And in what better way could he give back his thanks for the confidence and decision of Dr A.C. Chaterjee when he cast the decisive vote in his favour for captaincy of the 1952 side. The trophy was sent to the Olympic officials in New Delhi and Dr Rajendra Prasad, the first President of India, presented it to him in Rashtrapathi Bhawan.

R.S. Gentle, one of the most accomplished full-backs that India has ever had and who scored the winning goal against Pakistan in the Melbourne Olympics of 1956, was also a team member of the 1952 side that beat Holland, 6–1, in the finals. Though Balbir Singh scored 5 and K.D. Singh Babu 1, he credited the latter for most of the goals scored. Paying rich tributes to Babu in an article penned by him for the *K.D. Singh Babu Memorial Society* magazine issue (1981), R.S. Gentle laid down the bare facts of the 1952 win. Recalling the events vividly, he wrote:

> *India's top position in world hockey remained undisturbed in the last three Olympics, for, another player had now shaped himself on the lines of Dhyan Chand, and he was "Babu". The latter was compared to Dhyan Chand after his participation in the two Olympic Games of 1948 and 1952. Babu had the distinction of leading the 1952 team which defeated Holland in the final by a margin of 6–1. Babu had fantastic and fascinating stick work and he could mesmerise the best of defenses, draw them out and lay beautiful passes for his teammates to score. A unique character of Babu was his unselfishness so far as honour for individual scoring was concerned. He always played for the team; in other words, his skill and strategy on the field was inspired by one single objective, that his team should win. Babu could have scored 4 out of 6 goals himself against Holland in the Olympic final at Amsterdam, but he did not fall prey to this temptation; rather, [he] made sure that goals should be scored by passing to centre-forward Balbir Singh who fortunately never made any mistakes.*

> *Babu was a great leader of the game, a great player, a great sportsman, a great friend and a great storyteller. He had the knack to get the best out of his teammates. Though he was selected for the Indian teams for 1956 Olympics at Melbourne and 1958 Tokyo Asian Games, he politely declined the invitations with a desire to let other upcoming players have the honour of being a member of the team.*

Concluding the article, he further added:

> *Babu can never be replaced; he was easily the greatest after Dhyan Chand. His style and game of hockey has made him immortal. I wish we could have video tapes on Babu to train our youth. I remain one of his greatest admirers.*

Raghbir Lal Sharma, the left-out of the 1952 Helsinki games, had much to share with R.S. Gentle in an interview with *Swatantra Bharat* in 1978 when he said, 'Had there been no Babu, there would have been no Balbir.' Bobby Talyarkhan seemed to totally agree with the viewpoints of Gentle and Raghbir Lal Sharma after having watched K.D. Singh Babu play in some national championships in the late 1950s. His very vivid interpretations, comments and descriptions are contained in later chapters wherein Talyarkhan very vociferously advocated and held the view that if India was to retain its hockey supremacy at the Melbourne Olympics of 1956 and other upcoming events of 1958 Asian Games of Tokyo and Rome Olympics of 1960, there was no option but to ask K.D. Singh Babu to lead the side.

For Babu, hockey in particular and sports in general were everything in life. Even after being honoured with the Helms Award, he continued to work hard and kept up regular practice. So far as the issue of his having declined to be a member of the 1956 Olympics and later events is concerned, it is not true that he opted out to give others a chance. This was just a decent way of covering up an issue that was leading to mud-slinging. The plain truth was—the ambitions of some were scoring over talent and suitability.

Delhi Wanderers Tour of New Zealand 1955

Babu's dribbling is poetry in motion.

—*C.V. Walter, former hockey captain, New Zealand, (Sport and Pastime, 1955)*

World's Best Player in Indian Hockey Side.

—*Wairarapa Times-Age about K.D. Singh Babu*

The World Helms Award for the best athlete of Asia at the 1952 Olympics had propelled K.D. Singh Babu to the top of world hockey and every hockey fan now wanted to see this wizard in action. For many of those who had not seen Dhyan Chand in action and could not know what a wizard could do on the field, K.D. Singh Babu brought back memories of the golden era of hockey with a unique brand of delightfully clean hockey that only he and only he could play.

Before the advent of Dhyan Chand, hockey was mainly a hit-and-run affair. Dhyan Chand was the first to bring a change in the style of play. In the words of K.D. Singh Babu himself, Dhyan Chand was the 'inventor' of dribbling and body swerve which caught the opponents on the wrong foot. This style of hockey—dribbling and short passes—of players of the Indian sub-continent left the Europeans bewildered; the latter mainly depended on their speed. Hockey had become an artistic game, a game of jugglery and magic shows. It was the poetic movement of such artists that delighted the fans and often brought them to their feet in joyous applause.

To watch such a player wriggle past a ring of defenders in a serpentine movement, often throwing some of them off their feet, was what the spectators appreciated. For sports commentators of that time, what would only have been straight reporting in prose became poetic. After the end of the Dhyan Chand era, K.D. Singh Babu was the only artist who raised the game to such a poetic level that it was a treat for fans and a recipe for sports reporters.

On an invitation to play exhibition hockey matches, a team by the name of Delhi Wanderers visited New Zealand under the captaincy of Dr Gurcharan Singh. It included five Olympians who were also a part of the 1952 Helsinki Olympic team: K.D. Singh Babu, R.S. Gentle, Balbir Singh Sr, Leslie Claudius, and Raghbir Lal. Other members of the team were state players: Naresh Chander, Gur Dass, Pishori Lal Sharma, O.P. Malhotra, Suraj Balram, Jagat Inder, Balbir Singh Jr, Krishan Lal Sethi, Jaswant Rai and Gurcharan Singh.

Earlier, several hockey teams from India had toured New Zealand. C.V. Walter, former captain of New Zealand, who had also played against one of the visiting teams in 1938 and closely watched the performance of others as a student of hockey, paints a very vivid description of all the events. In his words:

> *The first appearance in New Zealand of Indian hockey players was in 1926 when an Indian army toured, playing 21 matches and visiting many small centres as well as all the major cities. The centre-forward was a young man named Dhyan Chand whose performances indicated clearly that he would soon become a legend in his lifetime. Although lacking the strength of a national team, this army group possessed enough talented players to demonstrate the skill and artistry which were evolving within the womb of Indian hockey and which were about to produce from then until the outbreak of the world war the greatest teams that the world has seen.*

Although these Indians were widely acclaimed throughout New Zealand, their influence was not universal. Their skills and their short-passing methods challenged the old concepts. Many recognised the worth of the challenge and accepted it; others resisted so that they might protect the ancient and honourable order of hit-and-run. Yet, there were enough players within New Zealand to provide respectable opposition and to arouse sufficient Indian interest to foster future contact between the two countries.

So it came to pass that in 1935, the Indian national team toured New Zealand. Its captain was Dhyan Chand, by now the greatest centre-forward of all time. With him were E. Nestor, Mohammed Hussain, M.J. Gopalan, Shahabuddin, Roop Singh, Peter Fernandez and others of less brilliance perhaps, but undoubtedly skilled. This team complemented, supplemented and enhanced the example of its predecessors. It confirmed the correct and true line of the game's development.

In 1938, the Manavdar state team visited New Zealand, which once again brought Mohammed Hussain, Peter Fernandez and Shahbuddin, and with them it presented the controlled efficiency of Feroze Khan, Shahnoor Khan and Sultan Khan. Summing up the tours from 1926 to 1938, C.V. Walter wrote, 'We who were young and struggling with the development of our hockey were enriched by these visits and forever doomed to the magic of the skill which was thrust upon us.'

In 1955, Babu came to New Zealand as a member of the Delhi Wanderers team of mixed ability because some of its players were not of a high standard. It played many matches during a wet winter on many appalling grounds in New Zealand, and much of the umpiring which it encountered was far from satisfactory. Its crowded itinerary gave its players insufficient rest and it was handicapped by many injuries. But its final record was very good and Babu was solely responsible for this. To me, he was the symbol of all that is great in Indian hockey and in the game itself.

At about the time that the Delhi Wanderer's team was about to land in New Zealand, the local press showered praise on K.D. Singh Babu and *Wairarapa Times-Age* prominently published a photograph of Babu along with a Tiger that he had recently shot in India. The photograph captioned 'Outstanding Indian Sportsman' created interest among hockey fans. Another headline read, 'World's Best Player in Indian Hockey Side'. Earlier, Helms Foundation based in Los Angeles had awarded him with the Helms Award for Best Athlete of Asia and the best hockey player of the world after his performance at the 1952 Helsinki Olympics. It was only quite natural that the press projected him as the greatest exponent of hockey since Dhyan Chand and hockey fans were eager to see one of the greatest in action.

Conditions for play in New Zealand when the hockey team visited in 1955 were at their worst. It was a wet winter and the venue chosen for exhibition matches was far from ideal for the type of hockey that Indians played. In the words of one of the members of the team, R.S. Gentle, the grass in the hockey fields was not cut and they were suitable only for grazing cows. After a few matches, K.D. Singh Babu refused to play anymore under such conditions as the fields were not suited for his style of game. Even C.V. Walter, who was covering the game as a reporter for *Sport and Pastime*, commented that at times, the ground was a veritable quagmire after heavy rains and sawdust was used in an effort to improve the worst areas. In one such match, the ground was so bad that when an attempt was made to roll its surface, the tractor pulling the roller got bogged and had to be shifted by a combination of mechanical and manual labour. Under such conditions, first class hockey was impossible. According to R.S. Gentle, one of the Olympians participating in the tour:

> *The conditions were not suited for Babu's style of game with the result that he drew some adverse comments by the officials and press of New Zealand, which were neither judicious nor in good taste, for an "artist" of Babu's calibre just could not do anything under those conditions. Babu was disgusted and he refused to play any more games in New Zealand half-way through the tour. Then in the last match of our tour of New Zealand, which was the fifth test on a beautiful ground and in bright sunshine, I begged Babu to play and show to the public of New Zealand what he could do with the ball. This match was against Canterbury side at Christchurch. Babu yielded to my request and showed his wizardry in this match; he dazzled the crowd with his stick work and although the host team kept five players to stifle Babu's attempts and to stop him, Babu eluded and dodged them all and could not be stopped. This forced the New Zealand press and public to change their opinion. And then they compared K.D. Singh Babu to the great Dhyan Chand. Heaps of praises were showered on him by the press.*

A news report of the match against Canterbury read as follows:

> *'Never since the visit of Manavdar team in 1938 have hockey followers in New Zealand seen such skill of attack as shown by Babu Singh and only the brilliant work of D. Goldsmith in goal blocked him.*
>
> *The Indians' front line worked with wonderful understanding, and the passing and ball control were at times uncanny. Babu Singh received round after round of applause as he weaved his way through the defense. Babu Singh had the crowd on its toes with his clever stick play.*

When mention is made of the Manavadar team that visited New Zealand in 1938, it is interesting to note that this was the same team, consisting of several stalwarts of 1936 Olympics like Mohammed Hussain and Gurcharan Singh, who had taken a beating at the hands of a young player of sixteen at the Trades Cup in Delhi. The player was no one other than K.D. Singh Babu.

Covering the tour for *Sports and Pastime*, C.V. Walter described his game in glowing terms. His two ornate articles, 'Babu's Dribbling is Poetry of Motion' and 'So Great Was Babu' became the talk in hockey circles. Describing his game against Canterbury, he wrote:

> *Well as everyone played in positions accustomed or strange, the match must go down in the history of New Zealand as the saga of Babu. I pause at my typewriter, at a loss for words. Never have I seen an inside-right play like him. He is the greatest hockey player in the world and objective judgement gives way to emotional pride and gratitude for the wonderful display of dribbling and passing which we were privileged to witness on Saturday, 13 August 1955. We who saw him will always remember the date and forever associate it with the genius of Babu. Ere half-time had been reached, the Indian team were cognizant of the magic spell being woven along that inside-right lane and were playing to him. No Canterbury player or a group of players could hold that dribbling, no one could check that passing. So great was Babu that not even the umpires could stop him, desperately hard though they sought to try at times. Babu raised a mere game on this day to an art and gave a new significance to our concept of hockey. This inadequate paragraph must be my tribute to a wonderful player and a wonderful sportsman.*

Calling him a summary of greatness, C.V. Walter wrote further:

> *K.D. Singh Babu is a player in the true line of descent that is skillful, artistic and progressive in Indian hockey. I run out of adjectives in trying to describe his superlative dribbling and the timing and geometrical accuracy of his passing. His knowledge of the game is encyclopaedic and his example and influence must be utilised to the greatest extent for the future development of the game in India.*

In the opinion of C.V. Walter, another great player on the tour was R.S. Gentle about whom he said:

> *I doubt if I have ever seen a player hit harder than R.S. Gentle but I shall not remember Gentle for his hard-hitting. Many people can hit harder and in fact, a large number of Europeans can do little else but few can dribble their way out of difficult situations with such outstanding ball control and few can feed their halves and forwards at the conclusions of such dribbles with passes as subtle and accurate as he. It is for these qualities that I will always remember him, because these are the real virtues of Indian hockey.*

C.V. Walter made some very keen study of all the players on the tour and felt that that the signs of decline were evident as compared to hockey of the past. Recalling the events from 1935 to 1955 in an article titled 'Hockey in New Zealand and the Indian Influence' published in the *K.D. Singh Babu Memorial Society* magazine issue (1982), he wrote:

> *During the 1955 tour, there were panic and fly-hitting under pressure, and there were passes which presented the ball to the opposition. There were*

> *those who could dribble but were unable to pass, and there were those whose stick work was limited. Hockey has marched backwards. Dhyan Chand, Roop Singh, Shahbuddin, Sultan Khan and Penninger could do more with a hockey ball on a rugby field than most of the moderns on astro turf. I think of a forward line consisting of Shahbuddin, Babu, Dhyan Chand, Roop Singh and Jaffar. I think of its operation on astro turf. I shudder to think of the manner it would sweep the moderns into the dustbin of history. Babu was a summary of the greatness of Indian hockey from 1928-1940.*

When C.V. Walter wrote that he was a summary of the greatness of Indian hockey from 1928-1940, he clearly hinted at the fact that from among all the players of the late forties and fifties, Babu was the only one who could line up in a forward line led by the wizard Dhyan Chand, and that too in the inside-right position which Dhyan Chand himself proclaimed as the most dangerous line of attack. That indeed he was the central figure at the 1948 London Olympics around whom all other players revolved around was proven when Berry Sarbhadhikary pointedly commented that 'Babu was the brains of the attack' and the Indian supporters could be heard shouting ever emphatically, 'Babu, Babu, come on Babu!' He played hockey like a chess grandmaster and could always pass the ball to the most appropriately positioned forward. This unique quality of his has also been described by A.F.S. Talyarkhan elsewhere in this book and it is said and widely believed that he was the only inside-right in the history of the game who could give a through pass from his position to left-out, thus leaving an entire defense helpless.

Recalling the events of 1955, C.V. Walter wrote that the Delhi Wanderers team had many weaknesses and most of the players could not trap the ball properly and sometimes gave passes that were either intercepted or went to the opposite players, but the deeds of Babu to some extent disguised the weaknesses of the Wanderers team. When Babu dribbled and weaved and feinted and passed, hockey made giant strides. Walters, who played as a centre-half against the visiting Manavdar team in 1938, further recorded that the 1955 Delhi Wanderers team was of mixed ability because some of its players were not of high standard. And given the many matches it played in New Zealand in appalling weather and ground conditions, with unsatisfactory umpiring and insufficient rest to its players, its final record was very good, thanks entirely to Babu.

The Delhi Wanderers played a total of ten matches against various sides. The tour opened up against Eastern Southland at Gore. The second match against Southland at Invercargill was played under pouring rain. In the two matches against Otago, playing conditions improved slightly and the hockey fans of New Zealand saw for the first time the fine stick work of the Helms Award winner.

After witnessing his magic on the field, C.V. Walter, who was covering the tour for *Sports and Pastime*, wrote a piece titled 'Babu's Dribbling is Poetry in Motion'. Then came the match against Horowhenua. The conditions were extremely bad and as R.S. Gentle commented, it was only due to the wizardry of Babu that we could beat them 7–1.

Various newspapers reported that in every match that the Indians played, K. D. Singh Babu was at the back of every move and every goal scored. The Delhi Wanderers players revolved around him. Describing the events against an Auckland side, one newspaper summed it up as follows:

> *The most conspicuous player on the ground was the inside-right, Babu Singh. He was always in the picture, wielding his stick like a magic wand in elusive and uncanny movements. The play seemed to centre round this player and he was responsible for most of the attacks. His perfect placing of passes and through shots allowed his other forwards plenty of room to work in, and most of the goals scored were the result of his work.*

The last match was played against Canterbury at English Park in Christchurch. The Canterbury side was the best of all the combinations that had played previously against the touring Indians and the conditions of play were excellent under bright sunshine. Never ever had the New Zealand public seen such a jugglery of stick work, amazing from all accounts, and the public and the press alike often rose on their feet to heartily applaud for they could not believe their eyes. This gamesmanship became permanently inked in the heart and minds of all who witnessed him play and C.V. Walter next write-up 'So Great Was Babu' in *Sports and Pastime* said it all when he commented that 'the match against Canterbury must go down in the annals of New Zealand hockey as the saga of Babu'. K.D. Singh Babu proved that he was the best hockey player of the world. Though the Delhi Wanderers team had other Olympic players who participated at the last Helsinki Olympic Games in 1952, it was he who really cornered all glory. His glorious display set a cat among the pigeons, for it set in motion manipulations to see that this great wizard who was still on top was somehow eased out of any future teams to make room for other aspirants who were overshadowed by his presence on the field.

The New Zealand Magic and Thereafter: The Real Story

There is no player in the world today who is as good as Babu was.

—C.V. Walter, former captain of New Zealand

While the New Zealand magic was music to many, it did ruffle quite a few feathers. This was a privately sponsored tour as the IHF coffers were empty, but it was seen on the same lines as the tours to East Africa in 1947 and 1951 just before the 1948 and 1952 Olympics. Though C.V. Walter opined about the Delhi Wanderers team being very weak, he also observed that the magic spell woven by K.D. Singh Babu somewhat disguised the shortcomings of the team. Some key players who were sure to go to Melbourne were being tested as before namely K.D. Singh Babu, Balbir Singh Sr, R.S. Gentle, Leslie Claudius and Raghbir Lal Sharma.

Sports and Pastime was the premier sports magazine of that time and the two aforementioned embroidered articles by C.V. Walter—'Babu's Dribbling Is Poetry of Motion' and 'So Great Was Babu'—created ripples that refused to die. A cold shiver ran down the spine of some association members and a player who dreamed of leading the side. Here, it bears mentioning again that even before 1952, attempts were made to sideline him from captaincy, but these attempts did not work. An Indian team to Melbourne without K.D. Singh Babu was unthinkable. He could not be displaced or replaced. And IHF President Naval Tata was a great admirer of Babu. Also, no one who mattered at that time could comment on the wizardry of this great player. Sports critics and hockey enthusiasts were keenly following all that was going on within the four walls of the selection committee room. But the lure to land the captain's role and lead the Indian team was a big temptation and a way had to be found to push someone else to wear this crown.

It was left to Jimmy Nagarwala to find a way out to sideline K.D. Singh Babu.

Nagarwala was pushing the case of Balbir Singh Sr, his favourite cop for the job.

And then came the stinger. Jimmy Nagarwala who was dead against K.D. Singh Babu leading the side started a smear campaign and spread word that since Babu was by then over forty years of age, he should not be considered for this job. Despite hectic opposition by Nagarwala, the name of K.D. Singh Babu was still emerging on top though. The strange thing was that though he was selected to be a member of the team, there was strong opposition to his captaincy. A player who had outshone every other player at the 1948 and 1952 Olympics by his shrewd playmaking and who was considered the 'brains of the attack' was asked to be a member of the team but not seen fit to be its captain. The tug of war continued. He was the sure choice of the critics and many in the selection committee. And then suddenly he withdrew from the team membership too under a disguised pretext, stating that now he wanted to give others a chance. This was not correct, but simply a decent way of pulling himself out of this contentious issue. The fact was that some key players who had aligned themselves with the Nagarwala camp created a division among the ranks of players likely to be selected for the Olympics. There were rumours of sabotaging their efforts to win. This was enough of a signal. K.D. Singh Babu wholly distanced himself and even refused to attend the training camp.

At the time, there was a trend in prevalence—any past captain did not consider it right to play under the captainship of a fellow player whom he had led and thus Babu quietly made way for Balbir Singh who saw it as his only chance to be seen in history of hockey as one of the captains. It was a Nagarwala gift.

K.D. Singh Babu was not the only one targeted by Nagarwala. A similar attempt was also made to throw out R.S. Gentle and the situation could only be saved when A.F.S. (Bobby) Talyarkhan cautioned the officials about the perils if Gentle was not included in the team.

The Melbourne Olympics said it all. The decline of Indian hockey had started. The Indian team was finding it difficult to live up to its reputation. Except for the preliminaries against lowly Afghanistan, USA and Malaysia, India had a tough time. The absence of K.D. Singh Babu as a star playmaker was immediately noticeable. Germany gave them a run for their money and only once in the later half could they pierce their defense and the winning goal was scored by Udham Singh.

Earlier, during the selections, R.S. Gentle was almost thrown out of the team and it was due to a smashing penalty corner shot by him that India bagged her sixth consecutive gold by beating Pakistan in the finals by a margin of 1–0. India only barely managed to retain her erstwhile glory, but in no way was it a convincing win as fans had witnessed in past Olympics. The forward line had failed and it was only India's defense that stood its ground to emerge on top.

K.D. Singh Babu always considered Udham Singh as a better forward then Balbir Singh and it was Udham Singh's misfortune that he missed the bus at the London Olympics due to an injury. Ironically though, Balbir Singh had no role to play in the 1956 win and it was more than evident that if India won the gold at Melbourne, it was largely due to Udham Singh's scheming and the glorious goal by R.S. Gentle that left the Pakistani custodian and backs gasping as he drove hard into the goal as only he could do.

Before I proceed further on this issue, I would like to refer to an instance from the neighbouring island nation, Sri Lanka, then known as Ceylon. A track event athlete, Duncan White, an Englishman who stayed back after the island nation became independent, competed in the 1948 London Olympics. He won a silver medal in the 400-metre hurdles and was later on awarded the Helms Trophy for being the best athlete of Asia at the Olympics. Recognising the great feat, his country decorated him variously. Apart from providing him a house as a gift, the government even issued a commemorative stamp in his honour. It was a fitting tribute to his achievement. And when after the 1952 games, K.D. Singh Babu was awarded similarly by Helms Hall, which in its citation called it as 'A Tribute to Indian Hockey', a smear campaign was launched to send him out of the field.

Hockey was now being played by those who had never held the stick.

Speaking about the genius of K.D. Singh Babu in an article titled 'The Uncomparable Babu' published in the *K.D. Singh Babu Memorial Society* magazine, C.V. Walter wrote:

> *In 1955, it was Babu who prophesised to me that a decline in standard has already started and that it would continue. I could see it for myself that there were players in [the] Delhi Wanderers team who lacked Indian skill at its highest level and who tended to substitute useless hard-hitting for that finesse and close combination which had previously characterised Indian*

> *hockey. I have always recognized Babu for his efforts to arrest the decline in standards and to restore Indian skills. There is no player in the world today who is as good as Babu was. Because of his personal ability, his knowledge of the game and his refusal to compromise with methods, attitudes, and views which would lower standards, he was at times [a] victim of criticism by those who lacked knowledge and insight concerning hockey and by those who were jealous of him.*

Going by what C.V. Walter said much later, his omission from the Melbourne-bound team was quite obvious. He always had his own independent view of things, which also included the composition of the team. As captain of the Indian team to Melbourne, he would have put his best foot forward in selecting his team and this was seen as a threat to the careers of some. The best hockey player of the world quietly quit the scene and refrained from any further international appearances. However, to show to the world that he was still good and better than the comparatively younger players, he continued to showcase his mastery in the nationals, so much so that he had again become a favourite, enough to be a part of the 1958 Asian Games and 1960 Rome Olympics teams after a lacklustre performance of the team at the previous Melbourne Olympics. But the drums of destiny were sounding a different note. Other nations were making rapid progress and the only way out for India to remain at the top was to bring the world-famous forward attack back into the team. Unfortunately, ego problems and blind favourtism were fully in play.

With the eElevent of K.D. Singh Babu, India was about to lose its shine, glory and supremacy in world hockey. That he was the master playmaker who created players by providing openings to his other forwards became clear from the glorious analysis of his game by the most celebrated and feared sports critic of that era, A.F.S. Talyarkhan, who always maintained in his vivid descriptions that Babu was the only trump card if India desired to remain on top.

The Knockout Punch 1957–58

Slogan writers suffering from the give-yourself-a-break and to-hell-with-experience phobia were given an anti-rabies injection by India's 1952 captain and winner of the Helms Award, Babu, at Lloyd Reclamation ground this evening.

But the best brains of FBI, if enlisted, would have been unable to put the "manacles" on this all-time great inside-forward. Words are inadequate to describe his wizardry. It had to be seen to be truly admired.

—*Hockey Correspondent*

Muhhamad Ali, the famous boxer, is credited with having once said that a champion is one who gives out a knockout punch right when people think that he is finished. While he was referring to his own comebacks, K.D. Singh Babu gave exactly the same treatment soon after he was indiscreetly sidelined by the IHF bosses just before the Melbourne Olympics because of vested interests. However, he continued his affair with hockey by making frequent appearances during the nationals and other championships. UP was considered to be a weak side as compared to Railways, Punjab, Bombay and others, but his mere presence was enough to demoralise the strongest of opposition. Time and again, he continued to dazzle with his stick, which was a treat for all who saw him in action. The press painted a vivid picture of his game. Though all the stalwarts of Melbourne games could still be seen in action during the ongoing nationals, it was only Babu who bagged all the glory. There was no answer to his attacking game. On many occasions, four to five players were deputed to shadow him, which was almost like half the opposite side trying to check his advances. When the defending players failed to check him, they resorted to obstructionist tactics and deliberately pushed him down to the ground, causing severe injuries. But there was nothing that could stop this maverick wizard.

The press came out with glorious accounts of his masterly display and the most vociferous of them all was A.F.S. Talyarkhan who laid bare the facts for all to read and understand. In his opinion, and as he and other sports critics saw him play, India had no choice but to ask K.D. Singh Babu to be a part of the Asiad 1958 and Rome 1960 teams if India wished to retain her old glory. Feelers were sent to him by the IHF to re-consider his decision of retirement but most unfortunately, he remained unmoved. The wounds of 1956 were still fresh and he was no one's rabbit. He was just there to flaunt his mastery and to show that the IHF were wrong when they sidelined him for the Melbourne Olympics. As hockey fans and sports critics clearly witnessed, he was the only player who could disturb the formation of opposing teams when a horde of defenders were made to form a ring around him, thus leaving the field open for his fellow players to make easy advances. And yet, as was seen by all, such tactics of the opposition had hardly any meaningful effect on his ball control.

Leading a weak UP side against Madras in the first national championship following the 1956 Olympics, he created ripples. Though UP lost to Madras owing to some very shoddy goalkeeping by its custodian Shyam Lal, and due to the absence of other two key players, Malhotra and Hem Prakash, it was again K.D. Singh Babu who made headlines. Despite the absence of some of his key co-players from the side, he alone created panic in the ranks of the opposition. Single liners from the press said it all.

Babu Beat A Rare Treat: Fans Applaud: Defenders Overawed

Slogan writers suffering from the give-yourself-a-break and to-hell-with-experience phobia were given an anti-rabies injection by India's 1952 Olympic captain and winner of the Helms World Award, Babu, at Lloyd Reclamation ground, this evening.

Making his first public appearance at Bombay's new hockey headquarters, Babu gave one of the finest performances by an inside-forward seen by regulars to this venue.

Although he carried a lot of weight in the wrong places—athletically speaking—he made it manifest early that he had not lost his magic touch.

Charmed Fans and Confused Foes

He charmed the hysterical fans with his dazzling stick work and superb ball control and conjured visions of a life-saving goal for Uttar Pradesh as he spread confusion and chaos into the ranks of a panicky defense.

Highlighting his game against a strong Madras team, the press wrote:

Despite the absence of his two other key players, Babu provided the only threat to their security and peace of mind. Though he could not settle down to ground conditions, he did give Madras a fright when he whipped his way around three or four defenders and scooped over the cross piece in the eighteenth minute. After Madras scored the first goal, Babu came to life and the match sparked with interest and excitement. Opposing centre-half Cotter was the first to panick. The commotion spread through the Madras ranks like wildfire as Babu wove and tricked his way through the panicked defense like a hot knife searing through butter.

Ring of Defenders

A ring of four men—two of them inside-forwards—were specially deputed to shadow Babu. But the best brains and brawns of the FBI, if enlisted, would have been unable to put the "manacles" on this all-time great inside-forward. Words are inadequate to describe his wizardry. It had to be seen to be truly admired. He then brought his wing partner into play with astute passes and some grand scoops and sent across four match-winning balls to the men who flanked him but his partners lacked the skills to turn them into account. Uttar Pradesh forced a spate of penalty corners but failed to equalise. Undeterred by the failure of his teammates, he then continued to attack and sent the ball to the roof of the net with a terrific shot but was unfortunately penalised for under-cutting. So panicky were the Madras defenders that they were seen rushing in to tackle more in desperation than anything else when faced by Babu. Poor Madras left-half Rashid had a gruelling and unhappy time and then Ghouse was brought in to help him against Babu.

...No man could have done more harm to undermine the good work of Babu than the poor goalkeeper. A replay would have been a sellout. You could not find a better draw card than the magnetic appeal of Babu.

As can be understood from the way he played against a strong Madras team, K.D. Singh Babu had the capability to destroy any formation. Instead of playing to their respective position, opposing players had to be shifted to counter him. The forwards forgot to attack. He had the unique capability of drawing opposing players towards himself which left the field open for his other forwards to move towards an open goalmouth. This is why he was known as the biggest playmaker. At times it was unfortunate that his teammates could not cash in and grab such opportunities. Given a side that could harvest his astute passes, victory was never far away. This is exactly what happened in Melbourne when against Germany and Pakistan, the Indian forwards could pierce effectively only once.

Then in the 1958 nationals, just before the slated Asian Games of Tokyo, he gave another knockout punch that shattered some of his detractors in the IHF hierarchy who, previously, had kept harping on about his age in an attempt to keep the slot of captaincy reserved for a favourite player of their choice. Unmindful of what was being said about him, hockey was what he wanted to play and he showed to his fans what it means to be a wizard. Sadly though, because of unwanted bitterness created by Jimmy Nagarwala, the 1958 nationals were the last time when hockey lovers saw the greatest hockey player of all time make his final appearance with a performance that dazzled one and all. What I write now is lifted from press reports of the matches as they appeared in various newspapers then. The most interesting accounts are from the pen of A.F.S. Talyarkhan who lambasted the IHF bosses for their attitude towards him and warned them of future consequences if K.D. Singh Babu was not included in the teams for Tokyo and Rome.

In one of the quarter-finals UP were pitted against Services. K.D. Singh Babu was leading his side. The first two matches were drawn and in the third outing, UP beat Services, 2–0. Not able to cope up with his wily moves, the Services defenders resorted to obstructionist methods, pushing him from time to time. In the second replay, he was roughed up badly, which gave him a back injury. However, he refused to take rest and went on to play in the third replay and despite a hurting back, led his side to a glorious victory. That he was a star attraction can be understood from the following press report of the first match:

> *Word of Babu's delightful display spread like wildfire and a goodly crowd turned out to see the Indian wizard in action. For the major portion of the first half, the Services adopted the right tactics to cut off the supply to the international inside-right. Inside-left Manuel functioned as a fourth half and shadowed Babu effectively.*

But this was not done based on any pre-arranged plan. Manuel soon settled down to play his normal game and Babu delighted his fans with some tricky long runs and intelligent passes to his winger, Caleb and centre-forward, Khuldip Singh. The 1952 skipper showed a fine turn of speed for short bursts. In the second half, Babu saw more of the ball and after the break, he came into life. His shrewd services had the Services defenders running around in circles.

The second replay was very frustrating for Services. The *Sunday Standard* wrote:

> *UP's source of strength in the attack was once again the wizard, K.D. Singh Babu. Not as dazzling with his stick as in the first meeting with the Services, he, however, showed what is stick work and the art of quick and clever passing. Babu made Shantaram Jadhav, the Services defense, tear his hair apart in fury as he repeatedly side-stepped and wove his way past him and his bewitched colleagues. Then he rushed back to push him down to the ground in the second half and was rightly penalised by the umpire, Jain.*

Commenting on the proceedings of this second replay which ended in a 1–1 draw, *The Times of India* correspondent went a step ahead in describing the wizardry of K.D. Singh Babu. Glorifying his game play as 'superb generalship', its sports correspondent wrote:

> ***Fast and Resourceful Uttar Pradesh Spark On Babu's Brilliance***
>
> *Sprightly Uttar Pradesh, remarkably alert and very fast on the ball, had to wait till the fifty-sixth minute for the answer to the Services' seventh minute goal although they tore great holes in the defense by their speed and skill and much the better of play at the Bombay Provincial Hockey Association floodlit stadium on Wednesday.*
>
> *Babu, the captain of the 1952 Olympic side, set the pattern of the Uttar Pradesh attack. Naturally slower than [in] his heyday, he showed that he retained his brilliance as a tactician and cut a path of glory with his magic stick. Shantaram, the opposing left-back, concentrated his efforts in curbing the ebullience of Babu but he was made to look ridiculous and had to resort to persistent obstructionist tactics to restrain the inside-right.*
>
> ***Superb Generalship***
>
> *Babu's superb generalship created a psychological fear in the minds of the Servicemen and some of their actions were born out of their desperation.*
>
> *When the lights were dimmed and the crowd melted towards the eElevents, the memory of the bubbling enthusiasm, the remarkable agility and splendid co-ordination of the Uttar Pradesh team and the exquisite stick work and brilliant strategy of Babu lingered on—the only lasting impression of the current championship.*

Commenting on the drawn match, Talyarkhan wrote:

> *The UP side were much superior in attack, even if some of their forwards waited on K.D. Singh Babu for inspiration. The ever wily Babu was always creating an opening and some of his forward passes were out of this world in timing and direction. Given one real sharpshooter as centre-forward, UP would be [an] odds-on bet for the championship. This tie easily produced the best flare of the tournament so far, and one cannot blame the Services for forgetting the ball and using the body to try and stop the famous Olympic schemer. Lying well back at inside-right, he awaited the pass of the ball from a colleague drawing back and the narrow paths through which Singh managed to steer the ball were as exciting as effective.*

When some sports critics opined that K.D. Singh Babu was now not as fast as he used to be and that he would not be able to keep pace with younger players, Talyarkhan retorted:

> *This is where some young reporters are making a grievous mistake—Singh has all his one-time mastery and guile and with the ball always in good control, it still takes him only split seconds to make monkeys out of defenders and then give his inside men the opportunity to have a crack. Considerably slimmed down from his last appearance in the nationals, Singh demonstrated that he is the cleverest forward in the country and if the selectors are watching the match, they have got ample evidence where one veteran stands in India's hockey today.*
>
> *...But there are ominous rumblings that one busybody selector is already going round spreading the diabolical report that K.D. Singh Babu is forty-five years old. I nail this lie but draw attention to this right now.*

In the third replay, Babu saw the end of the Services campaign. The press reported:

> *Babu's quick moving outfit improves with every outing. Once again, the gifted Babu delighted with his superb ball control and intelligent distribution. He ran circles round the opposing defense and Shantaram, the desperate one, was finally cautioned for a sneak attack on the Indian hockey wizard. In the forty-seventh minute, a penalty bully was awarded. Though Services skipper Nandy Singh had earlier failed to cash in on such opportunities, Babu showed the errant skipper how these awards should be converted.*
>
> *His lightning fast stick hypnotised Shah the defender and the Services were out of the competition.*

Watching him perform against the Services, A.F.S. Talyarkhan came out with a wonderful column that spoke volumes about Babu's wizardry. His pen upset many a stomach but what he said then and later on before the Rome Olympics became gospel truth. The decay of Indian supremacy in world hockey had begun because of the closed mindset of those who did not understand the finer points of the game.

Commenting on the UP versus Services match, Talyarkhan wrote:

> *UP made no mistake when ending Services' lucky survival in the tournament. Quality and speed told at the third time of meeting and with Babu distributing in fashion, which left spectators gasping with admiration, there was only one result possible in this entertaining quarter-final.*
>
> *Babu was, in horsey language, "on the job" and only went after the ball when he felt he would have the opposition on the wrong foot. It is very clever, this sort of dropping out of the picture for long periods, gradually shaking off shadowing defenders and then all of a sudden taking a hand.*
>
> *With those two magnificent wingmen, Caleb and Syed Ali, in top form, Babu could manipulate the ball as he liked and if UP did not score more than two goals—the wizard himself converted a penalty bully—it was because there is no first-time sharpshooter amongst the other two inside-forwards.*

Praising his game, Talyarkhan further added:

> *Babu never looks up before distributing the ball; he seems to sense the exact position of an unmarked colleague and the ball is deftly sent in that direction, never too hard, just forward enough, almost timed. Now we can see how Balbir scored goals for India which Babu served on a silver platter; no, that is not correct...*
>
> *On second thoughts, silver is too base a metal for Babu; let us say platinum instead, studded with those gems which once dazzled all world opponents.*
>
> *Here is a real drawing of defenders, but in a small compass, not the futile wide circling and drawing back which only enables men to fall back into other positions of defense. Into the thick of things goes the stocky artist and the greater the number of opponents piling on top of him, the quicker he seems to get the ball through. Then with one sure push, the ball goes through to right wing, or out to the other side. Here is one great brain left in our hockey, conjuring up memories of Feroze Khan, Johhny Pinto, Dhyan Chand and Roop Singh. Floodlighting is worth a hundred chips a second to watch this artistry.*

A.F.S. (Bobby) Talyarkhan who was the most fierce, fair and feared of sports critics of that time always used to headline his opinion column titled 'Take It From Me' with the closing line: 'Do you get me Steve?' This sentence had become his signature and was a poser for all concerned, specially aimed at those who were at the head of hockey affairs in the country. Writing for *Bombay Chronicle* and *Blitz*, he covered every important event, laid bare the facts, and no one could dispute what he wrote. Rather, his bitter pills were quietly swallowed and more often than not, he emerged right. He was one of the biggest admirers of K.D. Singh Babu; in him Talyarkhan saw the only hope for India at the 1958 Asian Games as also the 1960 Rome Olympics.

Reacting to the way Babu was manhandled and obstructed in the quarter-finals against Services, he wrote:

> *In every match that he has played, K.D. Singh Babu has got badly knocked about, very deliberately, and this is in a way a very painful tribute to older stars. Today's so-called top rankers are all hit-and-run, trip-and-push experts only, but is is poor gratitude to men who have shown the way to better standards of play. K.D. Singh Babu was a thorn in the Services defense. Curiously enough, when Shantaram gave up obstruction and started to play hockey, he made a better policeman to the player a large crowd had turned out to watch.*

The match against the Railways has gone down in the history of the game as the most grueling battle of all times. Events describe that UP were most unfortunate in many ways when they lost to Railways in the third replay. Though badly injured during the match against Services, in the final replay, Babu showed what he could do even during the dying minutes of the game when everyone thought all was over. The team was badly let down by the custodian and some bad umpiring. Despite all this, a packed stadium saw one of the biggest comebacks in the history of hockey when all alone, K.D. Singh Babu produced miracle after miracle which shattered the Railways, and if the Railways won, it was because they were favoured by the umpires and also due to some shoddy goalkeeping by Sethi.

The main focus of the semi-final was again Babu. One press correspondent wrote:

Inspiration, mentor and guide of the winners of the UP-Services match, Indian International K.D. Singh Babu told me after the match that it will be hard to beat the Railways. They have a very good side. Even before the semi-finals were to begin, Talyarkhan wrote:

> *The tidbit of the championship must surely be the evening's semi-final between Railways, the holders and Uttar Pradesh and on such occasions, I shed three quarters of the years I have lived and am yet as excited as any schoolboy to get to the ground early and work up enthusiasm to feverish pitch. To watch K.D. Singh Babu is in itself a treat this season and I dare say that one sure plan that the Railways had made was a means of stopping the wizard-like forward from advancing and distributing.*
>
> *UP's advance into the semi-final round of this championship has been [because of] Babu's ability to fox the opposition and I am sure to be scribbling tomorrow whether he got through or whether he was mastered. For me this tie anticipated a struggle between a set of very sound defenders and the only brain left in hockey's attack.*

As the time for the semi-final neared, K.D. Singh Babu withdrew from participating, owing to a back injury that he sustained during the match against Services. He had been advised complete rest by the doctors. Next morning's *Hockey Highlights* read:

> *The absence of Olympian Babu who has gained immense popularity in this year's nationals was immediately noticed by the crowd. Out came shouts of "We want Babu". This certainly is a fine tribute to an individual and the first of its kind in the city.*

Such shouts of 'We want Babu' by the crowd reminded one of similar shouts during the London Olympics when Indian supporters cried out 'Come on Babu'. Such cheering gave a clear indication that the supporters saw him as the only forward who could lead the team to victory.

Covering the match for *Bombay Chronicle*, Talyarkhan wrote:

> *Except for ten minutes in the second half, UP proved what a good side they are, even without the leadership of K.D. Singh in the semi-final of the championship. Looking back on a fast and exciting tie, UP had three-fourths of the roll of the ball and had they exploited to the full their whirlwind sorties in the first few minutes of the game, they would have won with a handsome margin.*

It was known only about a couple of hours before the match that Babu had been ordered by his doctors to take complete rest and lay off for some days. It was the nasty deliberate fouling of Singh in the quarter-final which occasioned this and when he obliged BPHA by turning out for the exhibition fixture, he paid the penalty.

In the second replay, though in terrible pain, K.D. Singh Babu disregarded medical advice and took to the field. His very presence on the field was enough encouragement for his colleagues while at the same time it rattled the Railways, the defending champions. The two press reports the next day had as much to say:

> *Babu showed no physical signs of a back injury and his presence hustled the champions into a near fatal blunder. Outside-left Champaklal was deputed to shadow the brains of the Uttar Pradesh attack and cut off his supplies. That was a wise move but only up to a point. Champaklal followed his instructions with a fanatical zeal and rare single-mindedness of purpose. He tailed Babu like a well-trained police bloodhound even when there was no apparent reason for this exaggerated precaution. Besides being injured, Babu took a hand with a few delightful placements, no one of which could be correctly exploited. When Champaklal fell back from the Railways left-wing to shadow Babu, it seemed the holders felt they might lose the match and in an effort to stop Babu, we again saw much obstruction, pushing and fouling to keep the Olympic veteran from making any headway.*

> *...One would imagine it is an honour for today's first class players to have a chance to face the old masters but the impression that many of us have formed after seeing how Babu has been mauled throughout the national, the younger set of hockey stars are admitting their inferiority, that they cannot possibly cope with such brilliance and therefore must block and bludgeon at all costs.*

With three players marking him, he failed to strike his wonted form in the first half but in the second half, this skillful artist could not be contained. Visibly suffering from pain, Babu bestirred himself and found gaps in the Railways defense. His inspired play brought out the best from his colleagues and they completely transformed the compleElevenon of the match and though 1 down early in the match, Caleb startled the champions with a late equaliser to set up a third replay.

In the third replay, K.D. Singh Babu again did not take to the field and he was replaced by Moolchand. In this replay, UP took the lead and then it was the turn of the Railways to look for an equaliser which they managed in the dying minutes of the match. Again the match was drawn, 1–1. A fourth replay was on the cards and there was tremendous excitement all around. It was a marathon semi-final as never witnessed before and all tickets to watch the fourth meeting were sold.

K.D. Singh Babu wrote in his personal memoirs that the biggest moment of his life was when he heard the closing whistle in the finals at the London Olympics, yet most people believe that the biggest match in his life was his dramatic display during the fourth meeting with the Railways in the semi-finals. Though Railways beat UP by 5–4, it was the day's line-up of memorable events for which Babu is remembered. If not for the lapse of their goalkeeper Sethi, who conceded goals which never were, UP had pulled a rabbit out of its hat. UP were also deprived of a chance to force a fifth meeting because of bad and biased umpiring.

In the fourth replay, the whole stadium was packed and spectators were expecting a grand display from K.D. Singh Babu. There were about twenty thousands hockey fans who had come to watch Babu's game. However, as events panned out, Railways took an amazing lead of 5–1 just fifteen minutes from end of play. It was because of some bad goalkeeping by the UP goalkeeper that Railways could score and one goal awarded to Railways was controversial. Thinking that now everything was over, the spectators started to leave the stadium. With defeat staring them in the face eight minutes away from the final whistle, battle-weary Uttar Pradesh, gaining strength and courage from an inspired performance by the celebrated K.D. Singh Babu, all but succeeded in forcing a fifth replay. It suddenly rained goals and the Railways were shattered.

Watching the match, Talyarkhan wrote:

> *Babu and his band of players came into life and one great move by Babu from right down the UP half to the Railways ring left everyone, on and off the field, marvelling in disbelief at the facility and speed of his stick. Everyone sighed at that time—"Oh for a sharpshooter!" That was UP's greatest need of the hour for Babu was laying the chances "on a platter" so to say. The Railways conceded three goals in the last ten minutes.*

Another correspondent wrote:

> *The spectators had all hopes of UP again equalising the match as they felt that this side still had life left while Babu and his magic stick were functioning. And UP's deed in the last ten minutes proved that they were right.*

With the Railways completely rattled by the game of K.D. Singh Babu and fearing that they might have to go in for a replay, umpire Fernandes blew the final whistle when one-and-half minutes of play was still left. The long whistle found UP in arrears. Sensing that the umpires had been partial to Railways, the entire crowd shouted down at them and the organisers. And their frustration could not be more eloquently expressed than in the little timely act by Babu. He picked up the ball and threw it across in the direction of Umpire Fernandes. Later on, Babu lodged a protest and the *Free Press Journal* published the below piece:

> *Gallant Uttar Pradesh, whose fantastic late rally almost gave them another chance to fight [it] out with Railways for a place in the finals of the National Hockey Championship, have protested on five points, but they have taken their defeat with a smile and do not want a replay. When approached by FPJ's representative K.D. Singh Babu highlighted some points to reveal the raw deal given to his team. Before the match started, K.D. Singh Babu had requested that Umpire Jameson should be replaced but it was not done. Also, that Balkishan Singh, who had been suspended from playing any matches, was included in the Railways team which was against the laid down rules. The fourth goal was controversial as the UP goalkeeper was pushed behind the goal line by a Railway forward, Champaklal, and the goal was awarded. He also pointed out that when Umpire Jameson kept time, why did Umpire Fernandes blow the final whistle? And lastly, the match was a minute and half short.*

A prominent newspaper came out with a glorious account of the match which appeared as follows:

> ***Victory for Railways, Glory to UP***
>
> *Brilliant Uttar Pradesh led by the wizard inside-right K.D. Singh Babu crashed to four goals to five in their third replay against Railways. But all glory to Uttar Pradesh. Trailing 5–1 midway through the second session and out of the match beyond all reasonable hope, Uttar Pradesh worked themselves up to such a fury that they rattled and undermined the morale of the champions into conceding three goals in the last ten minutes. That UP could ram home the equaliser in the one-and-half minutes left after they had secured the fourth goal was a strange quirk of fate. They had fought against hopeless odds with rare courage and considerable success. A chance to battle again with the champions was the least that they merited. Seldom in the annals of Bombay hockey had a side staged such a magnificent recovery, and seldom had a champion side paled into insignificance after what seemed like a thumping victory held firmly in their hands. To the undying chorus of "Come on Babu", the UP side responded with courage and hope and when Umpire Fernandes called time, there was not a single*

> *spectator who did not shed a silent tear for the fallen side. Yet, the story need not have been pathetic for UP, had goalkeeper Sethi kept his end. It was his failure in the final analysis that contributed to the Railways' victory. He could have stopped at least three goals, one being a perfect gift to Railways. It was something that could have shattered the heart of any side, but UP fought grimly on. There was a controversy regarding the fourth goal but Umpire Fernandes allowed it. If ever a team deserved to survive, if not a win, it was UP.*

So that was K.D. Singh Babu. In just fifteen minutes of play, he had almost turned the tables. Apart from scoring one goal himself, the other two were scored by his other forwards from astute passes given to them inside the striking circle. He had the great capability to draw the entire defense towards himself and lay goals on a platter. The main game plan of the opposition had always been to depute three to four players to mark him and many a times, when they could not check him, they pushed him to the ground in frustration, causing severe injuries. Unfortunately, as reported by Talyarkhan, his other forwards could not cash in on the opportunities provided by him.

Recalling the events of the match in an article published in the K.D. Singh Babu Memorial Soceity magazine (1981), Charanjit Singh, India Captain of the gold medal-winning team of the 1964 Tokyo Olympics, wrote:

> *I am reminded of this hockey match played in Bombay in the National Hockey Championship in which Babu was playing for Uttar Pradesh against the Railways. The latter had scored five goals against Uttar Pradesh and about fifteen minutes were left for the final whistle. Some of his enthusiastic supporters cried from the stands, "Babu, show us your game". Babu did respond to the "appeal" of his admirers and the remaining fifteen minutes or so, we saw him play such a superb game that he won the hearts of all. It appeared that his hockey stick had some magnetic effect which kept the ball glued to it with the result that his dexterous passes to his wingers resulted in three goals while he himself converted one. Had he been left with a bare two minutes more of the time before the close of the game, he would, in all probability, have sent in an equaliser into the opponent's goal, and maybe, he might have even sealed their fate with a clear win. Such was the command of Babu over the game. At the blow of the final whistle, Babu was lifted in a chair in the field by a huge crowd and taken out in a procession.*

That fateful day, the greatest hockey player of the world decided to bid adieu to competitive hockey. The grand *finale* reminded one of a similar round of thundering applause given to him way back in 1937 when, after his first appearance in a national tournament at the age of sixteen, he was carried aloft on the shoulders of a roaring crowd in Delhi. Being on top of the ladder for a full twenty-one years without any lean patch was no small achievement. And the press was the biggest beneficiary when he was in action. Unable to find suitable words to describe his fast stick work during the nationals, all that Talyarkhan could say was:

> *And finally, there is the jazz cum hockey fan who says that the only difference in the sticks of Babu and Morello is a drum.*

The gesture of the crowd was a befitting tribute to a champion of hockey. In the light of what Muhhamad Ali had once said, he gave a 'knockout punch' to his detractors to the delight of the spectators. An injured K.D. Singh Babu was still heads above his contemporaries and all talks about his age took a beating. He had shown why he was the greatest hockey player of the world. He had shown why he was honoured with the Helms Award for being the best amateur athlete of Asia way back at the 1952 Helsinki Olympics. The shouts of 'Come on Babu, show us your game' reminded one of similar shouts 'Babu, Babu, come on Babu' from Indian spectators at the London Olympics, and he was one who always responded on demand. Given a well-constituted team, he had magic in his stick and as per Talyarkhan, he was the only 'brains left in hockey'. He could lay plans like an 'army general', and one write-up which said that his presence on the field created a psychological fear among his opponents, reminded one of similar fear that struck among British army ranks when facing Rommel in the Middle East war. Even when he came out to play in the second replay against the Railways in an injured condition, his mere presence was enough to hustle the Champions into a fatal blunder when they deputed four men to follow him like police bloodhounds. He could make the opposition look 'silly' or make 'monkeys' out of them. He had the unique capability to tear apart any defense, disturb formations of opposing teams and lay open goals for his other forwards to score. *He was truly the 'Houdini of Indian Hockey' who dazzled all world opponents with his magic stick*. There was no stopping him and it was up to his other forwards to make good of the opportunities he offered them on a platter.

Twenty-one years later, on 19 April 1958, many a spectator shed a silent tear in appreciation of what they saw for the last time. A maverick wizard was calling it a day. His contemporaries, the players, and detractors, the IHF bosses—all had only one way out to checkmate him. By ensuring that he did not take to the field again. Their gain was India's loss. Great sportsman that he was, he obliged and refrained from participating anymore in competitive hockey.

Watching the other semi-final being played between Punjab and Mysore when Talyarkhan noted that Balbir Singh Sr of Punjab was unable to get hold of the ball, he wrote, 'Balbir Singh Sr was well shadowed and there is no Babu in the Punjab side to feed the sharpshooter; the result is that Balbir Singh has to get the ball himself and this is not his forte by any means.' By thus talking about the abilities of Balbir Singh Sr, Talyarkhan made it absolutely clear that Balbir Singh was totally dependent on K.D. Singh Babu to spoonfeed him inside the striking circle and this fact has also been shared by other fellow players, namely R.S. Gentle and Raghbir Lal Sharma, both of whom were members of the 1952 Olympic team.

After the nationals were over, the selection process for the 1958 Asian Games started. The magnificent performance of K.D. Singh Babu had caught everyone's eye but Jimmy Nagarwala, the chairman of the selection committee, was busy finding an excuse to exclude Babu at all costs. This is when he again started to talk about his age instead of extolling his game. As such, rumours started to spread and Talyarkhan hit back at the IHF bosses and tried to caution them about the outcome at the Asian Games if K.D. Singh Babu was not included in the side. Even earlier, before the 1956 Melbourne Olympics, he had specifically mentioned that Babu's wizardry was needed at Melbourne, but the selectors had made up their mind not to include him as they were hell-bent to pass on the captaincy to their own chosen blue-eyed boy. And the rabbits were out—India was barely able to beat Pakistan by a solitary goal whereas in the previous Olympics of 1952 they had beaten Holland by a margin of 6–1 all because of Babu's playmaking talents. Writing for *Bombay Chronicle* and emphasising the need for the inclusion of K.D. Singh Babu, he wrote:

> *Few will care to dispute the claims of K.D. Singh Babu on current form; after all, take it from me, his true age is much nearer 35 than the artificially created "45". Almost all the older players are on the decline, barring K.D. Singh Babu; how I wish we could drop the inelegant "Babu business". If K.D. Singh is at all keen, he should waltz into the India attacking line for the Asian Games. I am for all the younger players—with the 1960 Rome Olympics in view—but one veteran like Babu, now in top form, will provide everything India requires in the forward line.*

And then, finally, the names of players for the 1958 Asian Games at Tokyo were announced and the name of K.D. Singh Babu found a place in it. The team was supposed to assemble at Delhi on 28 April and it was reported that Swami Jagnath and Dhyan Chand would coach the team. Fed up with inner bickering which was affecting the morale and spirit of the team as also the repetitive tirade against him by one of the selectors, Babu finally made it known at a dinner in Bombay that he has decided to pull out of the team and refused to attend the camp. He felt that since there was no cohesion left in the team, it was not wise to be a member of a squadron that would not adhere to the basic rules of a flying formation. The all-out effort of Jimmy Nagarwala was to see that Babu himself walked out of the team as all his efforts to see that he was not selected had failed.

During the nationals, K.D. Singh Babu had again outperformed every other player and the press was full of praise for his game. In contrast, the performance of his contemporary, Balbir Singh Sr, was not even a dot on the vast canvas of impeccable performance records painted by the wizard. The resounding gesture of an impartial and spellbound crowd after the semi-final against the Railways when K.D. Singh Babu was lifted high on a chair and taken round the stadium with thundering applause had shattered Nagarwala's game plan. Adding to his discomfort were the explosive write-ups by Talyarkhan where he specifically mentioned 'Now I see how Balbir Singh scored goals which Babu laid on a platinum platter that dazzled all world opponents.' But Nagarwala was adamant about his plans and K.D. Singh Babu was adamant not to be a part of the team. He had risen to fame on his game, not by clicking heels before a cop. Once again, the field was open for Nagarwala and the heels of an aspirant for captaincy of the Tokyo-bound team clicked with thanks.

However, Talyarkhan continued to make the case for K.D. Singh Babu, and he tried his best to awaken the authorities to the dangers ahead after he learned that Babu had pulled himself out. In the two columns that he wrote for *Bombay Chronicle*, he emphasised the need for the great wizard if India were eager to register a clean win. But who cared? In the first expose, he wrote:

> *We have K.D. Singh Babu, whose form this season in Bombay has been a revelation. India's forward line should sparkle and if Babu goes to Tokyo, we can hear of Balbir Singh scoring goals as of yore. Balbir, now slower and less aggressive, is still the best first timer and with Babu feeding him, India still has a sure goal getter.*

In the subsequent column, he lamented:

> *I learn that the evergreen Babu is not keen to make any more trips to foreign countries. It is a great pity Babu cannot be made to change his mind but he is an independent sort of individual and clearly does not relish being kicked about, and not by any scheming selector. One feels that had certain things not been said about him in Bombay, he might have obliged this time. But it is too late to cry on spilt milk. Losing in the Asian Games may be dismal.*

Now the drums of destiny were beating hard and loud. No one among the authorities were prepared to pay heed to what Talyarkhan had been writing. When Talyarkhan closed one of his columns by expressing, 'that this time he might have obliged', he was clearly referring to a similar mauling given to K.D. Singh Babu just before the 1956 Melbourne Olympics. At that time, India had just managed to win the gold though they were badly shaken and bruised. In the absence of Babu, there was no one to split the defense and feed open goals. But history had no lessons for anyone. The team left the shores of India under the captaincy of Balbir Singh Sr. Balbir Singh Sr had a score to settle. He was determined to show to the world that what Talyarkhan had been writing about his dependence on K.D. Singh Babu to score was wrong. And now he was leading a team which was the best that India could cobble up in 1958. A win minus K.D. Singh Babu was a silent assurance to Nagarwala.

At the Tokyo Asian Games, India surrendered to Pakistan in the finals. Thirty years of supremacy was surrendered even when there was a chance to retain the old glory. Even though the team had many stalwarts from the previous Melbourne Olympics like Caleb, Leslie Claudius, Udham Singh, Balkishan Singh, Shankar Lakshman and Balbir Singh Sr, the forward line failed to click. In the words of Talyarkhan, there was no K.D. Singh Babu to split the defense and spoonfeed him. K.D. Singh Babu was the missing link between India and gold. The drums of destiny finally fell silent. It is not that Talyarkhan had the last laugh, rather, his famous outcry 'Do you get me Steve' reverberated all over. Earlier, no one believed him. If only Nagarwala had kept his mouth shut, there would have remained a ray of hope for the gates of victory to be erected once again in India. When K.D. Singh Babu pulled out of the team, it was a gain for Pakistan and a loss for India. It was the first time in the history of Indian hockey that gold was converted to silver.

The unpleasant defeat at the hands of arch rivals Pakistan owed largely to a faulty strategy on the part of its captain. The team was hardly devoid of talent but it lost because of poor understanding of ground conditions which demanded a totally different kind of planning. This is where captaincy counted and this was precisely the key difference between the leadership of K.D. Singh Babu and others of his time. When approached by the *Indian Express,* K.D. Singh Babu pointed out some basic defects that were responsible for the defeat. In his opinion, it was wrong to play two centre-forwards in the attacking line: Balbir Singh Sr and Balbir Singh (Railways). He felt it was a tactical blunder which starved the wingers and particularly Bombay's Chavan that considerably cramped goal-bearing moves. Referrring to the positioning of Balbir Singh (Railways) in the inside-left position, he further added, 'A natural centre-forward, he must have regularly clashed with Balbir Singh Sr, and Balbir Singh (Railways) suffered from the double disadvantage of not only being unable to create openings for others but also being unable to finish them when they were created by others for him.' Thus, spade work was sacrificed by this injudicious selection and the Indian forward line was rendered innocuous according to him. Referring to the style of play adopted by India, he said, 'We should have relied on long through passes and concentrated more on the wingers instead of inner forwards.' Considering that Pakistan also played the same type of hockey—short triangular passes—the long pass game was not only the logical answer but also the elementary one. In playing the short pass game, India found itself outclassed and out of breath because Pakistanis were a younger side with more stamina and speed. Lastly, he added, 'One more reason India should have switched on to [the] long pass game was because the playing surface in Tokyo was reportedly uneven. A short passing game on such a ground is always suicidal and that is what actually happened.' Ending the interview on an optimistic note, he said, 'I hope the lessons learnt at Tokyo would be put to good use before and during the 1960 Rome Olympics.'

His opinion about the wrong tactics used against a much younger Pakistan side seemed to align with that of Talyarkhan who had earlier cautioned that a young Pakistan side that played at Melbourne would reach its peak form by the time the 1958 Asian Games came around. And this is exactly why Talyarkhan had been trying to draw the attention of the IHF bosses to drop that 'Babu business' and see that he obliges this time. He had very boldly written, 'Babu goes to Tokyo, India is sure to win.' From the records it is also apparent that there was some controversy regarding the captaincy of the team. Talyarkhan wrote: 'While one cop favours Balbir Singh Sr, the other cop wants Udham Singh. But some say, it is Babu's chance.' Later on, it became more than apparent that the absence of K.D. Singh Babu turned out to be the main factor why India lost to Pakistan. No one of the forward line players of the 1956 Olympic side had the capability to split the defense of the opposition as K.D. Singh Babu used to do. Also missing was the 'superb generalship' for which K.D. Singh Babu was well known. Consequently, the performance of the 1956 Olympic team was below par and they just managed to retain gold.

His analysis about where India went wrong in Tokyo showed how he possessed all the qualities of a great captain who fully understood the finer points of the game. Every officer in the army does not rise to become a general. These commanding qualities were what distinguished him from the rest. And that is exactly why critics called him 'the brains of the attack', a facet that his other forwards exploited. K.D. Singh Babu was not only a wizard with the stick but he was also a mentor and coach of the teams that he led. His mere presence on the field would create a psychological fear among the opponents and they would get rattled, and at Tokyo, India missed his generalship. He was the rarest of the kind who understood the strong and weak points of the opposition and knew how to attack with characteristic chess-like moves. Former Olympian Syed Ali, who was coached by him, recalls:

> *K.D. Singh Babu had a divine sense to know about the strength and weakness of competing teams. In [the] Invitation Hockey tournament of 1974, our Sports Hostel team was pitted against Customs, Calcutta. We were losing by two goals. As I was playing as a left-out, he told me that if I am able to pass from the left side of the right half of the Customs team, then I will succeed in scoring. I followed his instructions and within a few minutes, I was able to score a field goal with my solo effort. Later on, we were able to score the second goal using the same technique through a penalty corner. Ultimately, we were tied 3–3 but in the ensuing penalty shootout, we lost to Customs. That day I realised what a genius he was, a quality that no player within my memory possessed.*

Fully aware of his genius and after getting a drubbing at the hands of Pakistan at the last Asian Games, the IHF turned towards him to coach and prepare the Indian team for the 1960 Rome Olympics. It was so strange that even as he was strategically sidelined from participating at the Asian Games, the IHF silently accepted that he was the only brain in hockey with a master plan for recovery. After the IHF made its decision known, the *Pioneer* came out with a brief but hard-hitting write-up echoing what Talyarkhan had been saying about K.D. Singh Babu:

> *The Indian Hockey Federation, alive at last to the mounting threat to India's supremacy in the world of hockey, particularly after the recent defeat at the hands of Pakistan, has decided to start a coaching camp where intensive training will be given to selected players in preparation for defense of the Olympic title at Rome in 1960. The IHF has been successful in securing the services of Kunwar Digvijay Singh "Babu" as a coach who at present is the Assistant Organising Secretary in charge of hockey and football for UP Council of Sports.*
>
> *The selection of Babu as a coach of experience of the Olympic team should not come as a surprise to those who have seen him play recently, and with his wealth of immense value in grooming the team. Inspite of his advancing age—he is in his late 30s—Babu has not lost vigour and dash and he is still peerless as an inside-right, the best the country has produced in [the] last two decades. It is a pleasure to watch him elude defenders, seemingly without effort, and create a first class opening. The reputation that Balbir Singh Sr has acquired as a goal getter has been largely due to Babu. Incidentally, Babu will be the youngest player to coach the Olympic team.*

However, later on, it came to be known that he did not take up the assignment and the job ultimately went to Kishen Lal, the captain of the 1948 Olympic team. The reasons for declining the offer were never exactly known but it was widely believed that some in the IHF were not prepared to give him a free hand and thus he saw himself out again. Stunned by his refusal, Talyarkhan wrote:

> *Internal politics is always very harmful and it is not a mere guess on my part that coming events may make or break the IHF. All the Services are taking keen interest in sports and the last two seasons have witnessed the gradual but sure spread of influence of high-ranking policemen in administrative spheres. I always favour the touch of Services' discipline in our sport but I drop a gentle hint that when top-ranking Service brass get into seats of authority, they have got to forget their official status. And finally, it is necessary to point out that hockey umpires must never use a policemen's whistle.*

The IHF were at their wits' end and were desperate to find a way out of this logjam. In an effort to please the critics and show that they were serious about retrieving the old glory, they then invited K.D. Singh Babu to lend an active hand in team selection. But the Augean stables of the IHF remained a tough task to handle. A selection committee for the 1960 Rome Olympics was formed comprising four former captains: Dhyan Chand, Kishen Lal, K.D. Singh Babu and Balbir Singh Sr. The last was included because of his proElevenmity to the chairman, Jimmy Nagarwala. As things turned out, there was a clash between K.D. Singh Babu and the chairman. In a battle of wills, Nagarwala wanted to prevail, and he wanted the selectors to abide by his choice. Sensing trouble again, Talyarkhan came out with yet another warning. Writing this time for *Blitz News* magazine (April 1959), he boldly criticised the composition of the selection committee and a part of his write-up is reproduced as below:

Indian Title in Danger at Rome

Who Selected Our Olympic Hockey Selection Committee?

One of the biggest problems we have had to face in international sport is what class of hockey team we send to Rome next year. Signs and portents are that there is a grave danger ahead with the dire possibility of losing a title we have held for thirty years.

I must keep on arguing that the four renowned players have all been forwards only in their time and the addition of a name which has only been found in Bombay police hockey teams does not indicate any cogitation on the part of the IHF. It looks to me a very peculiar selection committee and frankly, the composition is very dismaying. Let me tell you why...

No one can dispute the experience of the four Olympic players but it is doubtful if three of them are likely to dispute any matter with their chairman. This Jimmy Nagarwala has behind him a very dismal record of small-time interference and big-time swinging in the lead of Indian hockey and without casting any aspersions on him, I must say his chairmanship is not calculated to help free and frank discussions on selections. It is unfortunate that Ashwini Kumar, IHF President, is a brother of police officer and today's IHF set-up is made no one the healthier by the fact that Nagarwala's brother is the honorary secretary of the IHF.

When the National was played last in Bombay before the Melbourne Olympics, Jimmy Nagarwala for some reason or the other was responsible for queer propaganda against K.D. Singh Babu. Singh resented this and the result was Singh dropping out of the India team which badly needed his wizardry at Melbourne. The great player whose penalty corner shot at

> *Pakistan's goal retained India's Olympic crown, R.S. Gentle, has been another of the targets of the man appointed chairman of the selection committee. All sorts of accusations were levelled against the great Indian maestro but thanks to my exposure in the old Bombay Chronicle, things became too hot [to handle] for certain persons and the matter was discreetly dropped.*
>
> *Dhyan Chand, as I know him, is a thoroughly unassertive sort of a gentleman and not calculated to disagree with anyone who throws his unwanted weight around. Kishen Lal is another who, as I know him, is not going to dispute with anyone stationed higher in life (Kishen Lal was in Railways). Balbir Singh Sr is a disciplinarian, a copper who is always clicking his heels in the presence of an officer. And Nagarwala is an officer.*
>
> *This leaves K.D. Singh Babu and the last to be present when it comes to him and Nagarwala crossing swords. I must be frank if I am to place a matter of public interest before the public and assert that [the] composition of this selection committee is totally wrong and Nagarwala has no credentials to occupy the chair.*
>
> *I am going to say that in this selection committee there is every possibility that Nagarwala will oppose K.D. Singh Babu and I shall not be surprised if, under the circumstances, Singh, easily the mastermind in this selection committee, finds himself in a minority of one.*

Concluding his column, Talyarkhan wrote:

> *The only way out to prove my fears are unfounded is for the IHF to decide and invite the press when the final selections are made for Rome. This is undoubtedly a revolutionary suggestion but everything must be in the open where our representative teams are concerned. Do you get me Steve?*

Finally, and unpleasantly, India surrendered its supremacy in hockey to Pakistan at the Rome Olympics of 1960 too, all because the IHF refused to heed Talyarkhan's advice that they should stop that 'Babu business'. The battle was lost for the need of a nail.

Former Olympian Raghbir Lal Sharma who was a member of the 1952 team, while speaking to *Swatantra Bharat*, recalled that the feud between K.D. Singh Babu and the IHF bosses started way back in 1952 when the vice-captain of the team was being selected. While K.D. Singh Babu was in favour of Keshav Dutt, the IHF officials wanted Balbir Singh Sr. On the advice of K.D. Singh Babu, some members of the team including Raghbir Lal and Udham Singh voted for Keshav Dutt, but a whip was issued in favour of Balbir Singh Sr who was ultimately named as the vice-captain. For defying the orders of the IHF officials, Raghbir Lal was summoned before the Inspector General of police for indiscipline. As Raghbir Lal used to play for Punjab Police, it was taken for granted that he would obey their orders. Hence, this was the starting point of a bitter rivalry between K.D. Singh Babu and the IHF bosses that culminated in the smear campaign against him. He further added, 'K.D. Singh Babu was the only player who could draw the entire defense towards himself and feed open goals to Balbir Singh. He had the great art to dodge the opponents on both the sides whereas Balbir Singh had a poor field game. I wonder if a person and a sportsman like him would ever take to the field again'. Another Olympian of the 1948 Olympics, Amir Kumar said, 'K.D. Singh Babu used to say that attack is the best form of defense. He never relied on penalty corners and his attacking game was such that he could always create openings for field goals.'

Thus, the high-handedness of the IHF ultimately caused great damage to Indian hockey and K.D. Singh Babu just walked himself out, leaving the fate of Indian hockey in the hands of those who could not differentiate the colours in a rainbow.

A Rainbow Personality

If I can stop a full-blooded hockey shot from a close distance, the bat is too broad for me.

—K.D. Singh Babu to M.L. Jaisimha when asked how he could bat so well.

As a sportsman, and even outside the field, K.D. Singh Babu had a rainbow personality. There are innumerable amusing anecdotes one can recall from his life that uncovered his great all-round talent. Though modest, he had a very imposing and dominating personality. The high and the mighty of the society sought his company but he was equally happy when associating with the unequal. This became evident during the victory celebrations in his hometown, Barabanki, after the 1952 Olympics. As he was about to be taken in an open jeep for a victory parade along with the then governor of Uttar Pradesh, Shri K.M. Munshi, he amused the governor by jumping off the vehicle to embrace a rickshaw puller, Ghoora, who used to assist him in the times he practiced by himself. His liberal and accommodating style made him very popular among the masses and what added more flavour to his flamboyant lifestyle was his ever-present festive mood. Always dressed perfectly for any occasion, a pea cap or a hat used to be the most distinguished pièce de résistance in his attire, which made him stand out in the crowd. He had a big collection of such caps and hats which came from all over the world as gifts from visiting admirers. He was a generous benefactor and godfather to many sportsmen who sought his help to make a living. Helping others was in his nature and he demonstrated this amply during his sunshine days when he used to pass off the ball to a fellow player to score and make a name, even though he could himself have scored a goal instead.

Soon after calling it a day from competitive hockey, he took to other sporting activities. In a private conversation with me, former hockey Olympian Ali Syed said, 'He had a ball sense and could play any game with the greatest of proficiency.' Not many know that even during the time when he was making rapid strides in the field of hockey, he was also a university level football player as a centre-forward. In football, too, he could dribble the same way as he did with the stick. Later on though, he gave up competitive football after sustaining an injury during one of the matches. Then on the advice of some, he concentrated only on hockey. Football's loss was hockey's gain.

There is a very interesting story relating to his proficiency as a football player. In the 60s, he used to offer coaching in hockey to Sainik School boys in Lucknow. In the year 1962, a friendly football match was arranged between Sainik School and Colvin Taluqdars College on Colvin ground. K.D. Singh Babu brought his hockey trainees for the match. As a high school student of Colvin, I was also there in the spectator's gallery. The match started and soon enough, Colvin boys scored before the break. Until then, the maestro had been watching his team's performance from the gallery. After the breather, K.D. Singh Babu made a request to the sports in-charge of Colvin to allow him to participate alongside his trainees. Shri Birendra Shankar who was the sports in-charge at that time acceded to his request with a sly smile and commented, 'OK Babu, you are permitted to play, but remember this is football and not hockey, and what can you do at this age, our boys are too fast.' K.D. Singh Babu just gave a smile and took the centre-forward position. As the second half started, spectators were amused to see that he was churning out the same magic that he used to do in hockey. He dribbled past every opponent and with clever matchplay, he passed the ball to one of his strikers inside the circle for an open goal. The Colvin youngsters had no answer to his moves and as the match neared an end, the Sainik School boys were up. It was then that someone among the spectators who knew fully well about his football skills screamed at the top of his voice, 'Oh Mr Birendra Shankar, whom have you permitted to play! Did you not know that he was a top-class university level centre-forward in football?' I am unable to recollect what the end result of the match was, but all that is still fresh in my mind is that after the match, the Colvin teachers made a lot of protests amid laughter.

And it was not only hockey and football that K.D. Singh was a pro at; he could take up practically any sport like a duck takes to water. In the year

1962, I happened to join a cricket coaching camp being held by someone named Shri Prithvi Raj at what was then known as Central Sports Stadium (now K.D. Singh Babu Stadium) at Lucknow. Shri Prithvi Raj was a sports officer in-charge of cricket and a coach par excellence. While he held his camp in one corner of the stadium, at the same time K.D. Singh Babu used to hold his hockey camp in another corner. During the month-long duration of our camp, K.D. Singh Babu would invariably walk towards the net with a stick in hand, challengeing Shri Prithvi Raj to try his best bowlers while he batted with a hockey stick. He would announce that if any bowler could clean bowl him, he would offer sweets to the entire camp. The best fast bowlers and spinners were then pressed into action but to the amusement of all, he would very easily deflect every ball and no bowler could uproot the wickets. What was even more surprising was that he never even wore leg guards! Later on, he became a regular at the camp and took some fine tips from Shri Prithvi Raj. Even though Shri Prithvi Raj was a sports officer serving under Babu, the latter would always address him as 'Sir'. Once, when Shri Prithvi Raj mildly protested that he felt embarrassed when Babu, who was his boss, addressed him thus, Babu retorted that he would continue to address him that way as he was his guru in cricket. Though Babu had taken up cricket in the dusk of his life, he nevertheless showed that he could have been a great showman in cricket too. He was a quick learner and though he could swing the ball both ways, batting remained his main strength. At that time, Sheesh Mahal cricket tournament had become a regular summer feature in Lucknow, and as the tournament became more popular, some prominent cricketers of the country also started to participate as members of various participating teams. M.L. Jaisimha and Farouk Engineer were the most regular players and once, even Chandu Borde and the legendry Mushtaq Ali made their appearance. It was during one such tournament that the great Bishen Singh Bedi showed his class as a member of Vijay Club of Amritsar and if I remember right, he delighted the crowd with his deft bowling when he crowned himself with the only hat trick the tournament ever recorded.

Playing alongside seasoned and accomplished cricketers of the country and the state, K.D. Singh Babu notched up many big scores which also included an undefeated double ton (236 not out) and giving him company was Shambu Puri, a Ranji Trophy player who himself was a top-class fast bowler. M.L. Jaisimha and Farouk Engineer came to be rather intimate with him and very often they would stay with him at his residence. Once when Jaisimha questioned, 'Babu, how can you play so well?' the latter replied, 'If I can stop a full-blooded shot in hockey from a close distance, the bat is too broad for me'. And indeed, it was so. My golfer friend Veerendra Kapoor, who was a former cricket captain of Colvin College cricket team, recalls, 'I used to think that I was a good spinner but Babu sahib lifted me for the longest six of the tournament and that too out of the stadium.'

Racket games came easily to him, whether it was tennis, badminton or table tennis. He was the most regular tennis and badminton player at the Oudh Gymkhana Club, Lucknow. After finishing office work in the evening and whenever he could snatch some time from his other commitments, a game of tennis was what he enjoyed before calling it a day. For many consecutive years, he remained the district champion in tennis and badminton. M.L. Jasimha was also a very good tennis player and during his summer visits to Lucknow to participate in Sheesh Mahal tournaments, both he and K.D. Singh Babu would go to the gymkhana to try each other out.

One dignitary who always sought to play tennis with him was former President Shri V.V. Giri when he was the governor of Uttar Pradesh. At the time, the governors of the state always moved to Naintal during summers. Most often, K.D. Singh Babu would also be there to participate in local hockey tournaments which were organised on the flat. The 'flat', as mentioned here, is a fine gravel field by the side of the Nainital lake, about the size of a hockey field, and hockey and football matches during summers used to be a big attraction. Apart from making brief appearances in some matches to delight the crowd, K.D. Singh Babu used to spend a lot of time fishing in the lake. And playing tennis with His Excellency was an honour. Quite often, when he got late to make it to Raj Bhawan, His Excellency would send an emissary with a car to fetch him as His Excellency enjoyed playing with him alone, and no one else. Whenever other senior staffers of the camp would request His Excellency for a game, he would always reply, 'No, I will only play with Babu.'

In the year 1969, when Shri V.V. Giri visited Lucknow during his presidential tenure, the then governor, Shri Akbar Ali Khan, sought to know from him if he had any pre-set agenda in mind. 'Oh,' said the President, 'I just want to meet Babu. Invite him over for tea with me in the evening.' The message was immediately conveyed to K.D. Singh Babu that the president wished to see him that evening. At the time, since Major

Dhyan Chand, on a short visit to Lucknow, was staying with him, K.D. Singh Babu felt that it would be unwise if he went alone, leaving the wizard back home. So Babu made a request with the staff of Raj Bhawan to kindly inform the president that since Major Dhyan Chand was staying with him, he would be happy if the invitation could be extended to the wizard as well. The invite was quickly modified and then the duo met the president over tea, sharing with him the glorious past of Indian hockey. Such incidents spoke volumes about Babu's greatness.

In Lucknow circles, he also enjoyed the company of a group of friends who were keen golfers. Every day, he used to listen to their stories of how well they played the game of golf and what an entirely different game it was. Prominent among them were the late Shri Ram Advani, the founder member of Lucknow Golf Club, as also Satendrajit Singh and Yogendrajit Singh, the owners of the famous Carlton Hotel in Lucknow. After many such sittings of gossip and bravado, one day, Babu decided to try this game. There is a very interesting story about his first day on the golf course as narrated to me once by Shri Ram Advani. He recalled:

Babu expressed his desire to play golf and we all promptly invited him to try his hand. On day one, we gave him a lesson about the stance and the swing. Next, he put the ball on the tee, took a stance and swung the club. To the amusement of everyone present there, he totally missed connecting the ball. He then made a few more attempts but failed to get a proper connection. As everyone laughed, I told him, "Babu, you may be the greatest hockey player of the world but remember, this is golf, which is an entirely different game."

"Oh I see," he shot back, "now let me play the way I can." Then he added, "I cannot understand why you people want me to stand still while addressing the ball."

Next, he rolled the ball on the ground, took a few steps back and then all of a sudden, approached the ball at a fast pace in typical hockey-like fashion and then what everyone saw was a fantastic shot that took everyone by surprise. All through his golfing days, he played the same way, defying the basics of the game and soon, he became a single handicapper. Some of the old caddies of the club who had seen him play told me that he used a two iron for all purposes except putting. As I am also a very keen golfer, my father, who was immediately younger than Babu, asked me to teach him something about golf. As I was trying to tell him whatever little I knew, Babu quipped, 'What fun, you people are really fussy about the stance!'

Babu used to play the game just as he played hockey and he never failed! Old timers in the club still talk about his adroitness that defied logic, and again and again it was Ram Advani who kept telling him, 'Babu, you cannot be Gary Player', but he stuck to his own methods and showed everyone how a great sportsman can make use of unconventional methods.

Complete sportsman that he was, he once showed us his skills in table tennis too, way back in 1975. We the youngsters in the family used to pass our evenings playing table tennis at our residence and we all pooled in money to buy a nice table. He knew about this and suddenly one day, he dropped in to participate. He then enquired as to who among us was the best player? One of my cousins, Dhruv Raj Singh, was an ex-captain of the table tennis team of Lucknow University. So it was only natural that he proudly came forward and disclosed his credentials. 'So you are the best player of the lot and former captain of Lucknow University?' Babu asked. Dhruv Raj Singh smiled and nodded in affirmation. 'Okay, then let us have a game and let me see how good a player you are,' Babu replied. Dhruv Raj Singh had been using the finest Barna racket available at that time and all that was available to Babu was an outdated one borrowed from us. The match started and Dhruv Raj Singh tried to impress him with smashes and spins. But as we watched, nothing worked. Every smash was returned and every spin countered. Ultimately, Dhruv Raj Singh lost by a good margin. Putting down the racket on the table, Babu laughed and said, 'Learn more about the game, D.R. Singh.' The camel was dwarfed by the mountain.

Lest you think that field or indoor games alone were K.D. Singh Babu's forte, the great thinker that he was, it came as a big surprise for some when he once beat Munno DiElevent, an all-India ranker, in chess. Munno DiElevent was also a good hockey player and later on, he also took to coaching hockey. After Munno DiElevent lost the first game, he challenged Babu to another game. 'No,' Babu said though, 'no more games.' When Munno DiElevent asked him the reason for not playing any further, he jokingly replied, 'Well Munno, because I want to remain one up on you.' What he could do in hockey, he did in chess too. Here, one is inclined to believe what former hockey player Syed Ali Sibtain Naqvi had said, 'His dribbling and ball control was amazing. It was as if he had a sixth sense about the game, he could literally predict the moves.' He played hockey like chess and chess like hockey and this ease of jugglery totally baffled his opponents.

A multi-faceted personality like him is very hard to imagine. He was a phenomenon that surpassed this world. His office was always a beehive of activity right from morning till evening. Always surrounded by people who approached him for various needs and recommendations, he never disappointed anyone. Countless sportsmen benefited by finding their livelihood, thanks to him. His recommendations landed them jobs, be it in the customs, railways or police. Taking full advantage of his position as a member of the Railway Board, he pushed many careers forward; the Indian Airlines hockey team comprised varied members, all of whom had been his trainees.

K.D. Singh Babu was very well aware of the pathetic conditions of sportsmen at that time in the country as he had himself passed through such a phase. Briefly in the late 60s, he gave up his position as Organising Secretary of UP Sports Council and joined a hunting company by the name of Allwyn Mercury owned by Vidya Charan Shukla, a political giant of Madhya Pradesh, in the capacity of an advisor, which he thought would be more lucrative financially. In 1967, matters changed all of a sudden. Chaudhary Charan Singh had taken over as Chief Minister of Uttar Pradesh and on the very first day, he appointed K.D. Singh Babu as Director, Sports. His personal experience of hardship, even after reaching the highest rung of the ladder, found a permanent place in his heart. As his credibility and position in government circles grew, it was he who recommended to the government that sportsmen who had excelled at a certain level be given pension, and this scheme is being followed even today.

A glaring example of his sympathetic attitude towards sportsmen is the story of famous yesteryear tennis player Ahad Hussain who made it to Wimbledon. Ahad Hussain came from a poor family of Barabanki, the hometown of K.D. Singh Babu. Once, he was out on a shoot, when he suddenly saw an old man picking up dry twigs in a mango grove to light a fire. Babu recognised him immediately and went up to him. Ahad Hussain was in pathetic condition. Babu embraced the man and asked him to come to Lucknow and get in touch with him there, for he wanted to help a man who had brought glory to the country. For him, status meant nothing. For him, it was always the person who mattered, and more so if the person had been connected with sports at any level.

Sporting activities at any level always attracted him and he used to be more than happy playing with youngsters. On one such occasion, he passed by a small school in a village where he saw youngsters playing hockey. He stopped the car and watched them play for a while. After a few minutes, he entered the field and requested one of them to let him have his stick. The youngster obliged and then he started playing with the rest. At first, the village children had no idea that one of the all-time greats of the country was playing with them, but they were certainly amused as no one could take away the ball. All of a sudden, one of them recognised him and asked, 'Are you K.D. Singh Babu about whom we have a lesson in our textbook?' He smiled back and said yes. The headmaster was called and a holiday was declared in honour of his visit.

Soon after the 1971 war with Pakistan, some prisoners of war were camped in Bareilly. Among them was some lesser known hockey player from Pakistan. Worried to know about his welfare, his family contacted their relatives living in Lucknow. Since this POW was a hockey player, his Lucknow-based relatives approached K.D. Singh Babu to help find out about him. Never one to say no to anyone, Babu promised to find out about his wellbeing. And then one day, he drove off to Bareilly. At that time, I was living with my father in Bareilly. Asking me to accompany him, he drove to the camp. At the highly fortified gate of the camp, he sent his credentials to the officer in charge of the camp, requesting a meeting. We were allowed entry and ushered into the office of the in-charge who turned out to be a colonel. Entering a sensitive area such as a POW camp during the heightened tension between the two countries was near impossible for any other person, but K.D. Singh Babu's name worked. Tea followed, and then he let the colonel know about the purpose of his visit. Though he was not allowed to meet the prisoner personally, the colonel was pleased to send a subordinate to convey to the concerned prisoner that on the request of some of his relatives in Lucknow, K.D. Singh Babu had come to enquire about his welfare. The prisoner conveyed with a big thanks that he was being looked after well and was keeping good health.

Apart from showing his skills in the field of sports, angling and hunting were Babu's favourite weekend pastime. His paraphernalia of fishing gears was a very varied collection meant for different conditions and he would travel far distances like the terai of Nepal and Kumaon for Mahseer fishing. Randhir Singh Gentle, the greatest deep defender of the Indian Olympic team who scored the winner against Pakistan at the 1956 Olympic Games, used to be with him on many such occasions. A daring big game hunter with intricate knowledge of the ways of the wild, he was always very quick and accurate with the gun. Although it sounds very inappropriate to mention it now, owing to present-day conservation policies, the six tigers that he shot under difficult conditions had their own wonderful story to tell. The most remarkable of all was the case of a pair of cattle lifting tigers whom he shot on demand and he felled them both in a split second, not giving them any chance to escape.

He was a crack shot, totally unbelievable, whether it came to shooting flying partridges or waterfowl. Even when shooting waterfowls in twilight hours, he would hardly miss. His favourite weapon was a 25–inch barrel Grand Prix which was extremely suitable for hunting partridge and waterfowl. There is a very interesting account of how he managed to get this beautiful gun, but I will come to it later on in this chapter. Appreciating his marksmanship and rapidity, Mr K.K. Das, ICS and former chief secretary of Uttar Pradesh, who had almost become his permanent company on such shoots, presented him with a Labrador named Queeny. K.D. Singh Babu used to take her with him on every such shoot and very soon she developed into a top retrieving dog. Like her master, Queeny never missed any bird and many a times, she would brave cold and deep waters to retrieve a fallen fowl. She was equally good in flushing out partridges. But poor Queeny had a very tragic end. She got electrocuted, and that day her master wept, for he had lost a good and loyal companion.

What distinguished him from other sportsmen of his time were his multifarious activities and interests that made him the cynosure of all eyes. Dignitaries and high-profile people from all walks of life were his company and he knew how to conduct himself on any occasion. In 1969, he happened to go to Kanpur to watch the India-Australia test match. It was Gundappa Vishwanath's debut and Tiger Pataudi was leading the side. Having seen him sitting in the VIP pavilion, Pataudi came over to him for a short round of gossip during the lunch break. The two of them discussed hunting and then Pataudi expressed his desire for a waterfowl shoot with him, to which he agreed. Pataudi dispatched his orderly to Bhopal to get his gun which was custom-made for him as he could use only one eye following an injury that he had sustained in an accident years before. After the test was over, Pataudi joined him in Lucknow, accompanied by wicket keeper Inderjit Singh. Later on, Babu told us that despite being handicapped, Tiger was a terribly good shot.

In an interview given to a prominent newspaper in sweet remembrance of his days with K.D. Singh Babu soon after he passed away in March 1978, Mr K.K. Das narrated a very interesting story.

'I and Babu were invited by His Excellency King Mahendra of Nepal for a shoot in the Nepal terai. At that time, I was Commissioner at Lucknow. My counterpart in the Nepal government, the Anchaladhish, was deputed by His Excellency to look after us during our stay. At that time, India-Nepal relations were a bit strained over some petty matters and I was very keen to see that the relations took a turn for the better. Knowing full well that the Anchaladhish was not a good shot, I indicated to Babu that he must do something so that he is pleased. Babu got the hint. We were riding on elephant back and the beat soon started. Soon after, a hog deer ran out of the thickets. Both Babu and the Anchaladhish raised their guns and aimed at the running deer. Babu waited, but at the same time, he kept an eye on the host. The moment the Anchaladhish fired, Babu timed the shot and the deer dropped dead. It was only Babu who could have done something like that—firing simultaneously and making it look as if our host got it bang on target. It was a difficult shot as the deer was visible only for a few seconds. Later on, Babu congratulated the Anchaladhish for the fine shot, but I knew it was Babu who had shot the deer as only he could have put the bullet in the right place on a fast-running deer. The Anchaladhish was very pleased and so was I. But the credit went to Babu.

The story of his English Grand Prix 12-bore gun is very interesting. Once, he came to know that Raja Bajrang Bahadur of Bhadri, with whom he had very pleasing relations, had an exclusive gun. And he wanted to possess this gun at any cost. So one day, he paid a visit to the Raja and after the initial exchange of greetings, the discussion narrowed down to various top-class guns like Perdy and Churchill. Then coming down to his secret mission, he made a request to see his gun. Totally unaware of what fate awaited him, the Raja asked his servant to bring the gun. After examining and secretly appreciating it, Babu put it back on the table and gave very ordinary comments about its quality. The comments were intentional, so as not to alert the Raja. He then changed the topic and flattered the Raja by extolling how influential the Raja was in political and bureaucratic circles. Convinced that now the Raja was enjoying all this praise for his exalted status, he requested the Raja to pen a letter of recommendation to the district magistrate of Lucknow for him.

Stunned by his request, the Raja shot back, 'What, me making a request for you to the district magistrate! Do you not know him personally? I believe you do.'

Not to be deterred by this counter query, Babu succeeded in convincing Raja Bajrang Bahadur that his recommendation would really make a difference. The Raja got his letterhead out and asked him what to write.

'Well,' replied K.D. Singh Babu, 'you need not bother what to write, just put down your signatures on the bottom and I will get it typed.'

As the Raja consented to his request, Babu exploded with laughter and thanked him for gifting the gun to him. The Raja also laughed and said, 'Well, I had an inkling that you wanted this gun, so why all this drama!' He then penned the transfer letter himself and the gun changed hands. Much later, after having used this gun intensively for a long period and after it had lost its accuracy, Babu sold it off to a local gunsmith. One friend of mine, Rashid Kidwai, had been intending to buy a good gun. He was shown this gun by the shopkeeper. When he had almost decided to buy it, the shopkeeper told my friend that he is lucky to buy it as its previous owner was K.D. Singh Babu. The moment he heard the name, he put it down and refused to buy it. When the shopkeeper asked him the reason, he replied, 'If a connoisseur like him has sold off this gun, then there is nothing left in it.' It was absolutely true as no one knew about guns as much as Babu did.

Every year, Mr K.K. Das used to request me and my uncle Kr Shukdeo Singh 'Mohan' to help him prune his roses as we both were quite accomplished in this task. Once, after finishing pruning, while we and Mr and Mrs Das were having tea in the garden, some Labrador puppies suddenly appeared in front of us. As we were appreciating the litter, Mrs Das revealed that the best puppy has been taken by K.D. Singh Babu. Surprised, my uncle asked Mrs Das as to why they gave it to Babu. A smile appeared on Mrs Das face and she said, 'Oh Mohan, who gives it to Babu, he just takes!' We all joined in great laughter, being all too familiar with Babu's inimitable style of getting what he desired and for most people, it was a matter of pride to oblige him.

The most memorable and interesting duel that I happened to witness was with my father. In 1968, my father was posted to Kathmandu on deputation where he purchased a Ford Mustang. Back to India after the deputation was completed, he made a brief halt at Lucknow. K.D. Singh

Babu saw the iconic car with open appreciation in his eyes and then asked my father for the keys. My father made great efforts not to let him drive the car but nothing worked and finally K.D. Singh Babu drove off to his office driving the Mustang. Back in the evening, he tried to convince my father to give the car to him. But my father did not relent. He then turned towards me and said, 'Son, why can't you ask your father to give the car to me.'

'Well,' I replied, 'it is between you two to decide, who am I to intervene?'

He jocularly replied, 'You see, when your father drives the Mustang, onlookers say that someone is going in a Mustang but when I was driving the Mustang today, they said, "Look Babu is driving a Mustang". Don't you see the difference?'

And then he gave back the keys to my father with a comment, 'If you again give the keys to me, you shall never get back the car.'

Later on, he said to me, 'No, I was just joking and rather, I am happy that he has got a world-famous car.'

In the truest sense, Babu himself was an advertiser's precise model and fans used to copy his style all the time.

When a cultural organisation by the name of Ravindralaya was launched in Lucknow, he was the obvious choice to be its first president given his widespread fame. He was well-known in Bollywood circles right from the time of his active playing days and as A.F.S. Talyarkhan had mentioned, 'Bombaywallahs turned out in large numbers just to watch one man play, and that was K.D. Singh Babu.'

The biggest beneficiary of his celebrity status was his peon, Ramdin. Sitting on his stool at the entrance to his office room in the stadium, he would put every visitor through rigorous questioning before allowing entry. Once, when film star Karan Diwan came to meet K.D. Singh Babu, his first encounter was with Ramdin. When Karan Diwan requested for a meeting, Ramdin shot back, 'No, sahib is taking rest and I cannot allow you to enter.' When Karan Diwan disclosed his identity, Ramdin, who was a cine addict, suddenly jumped to his feet and took a close look at him. Ramdin had seen many of his films. Correcting himself, he said, 'Oh so you are Karan Diwan and you can most certainly go in!' However, Ramdin extracted a promise from him that Karan Diwan will have to pose with him for a photograph. Karan Diwan readily agreed. As he entered to meet K.D. Singh Babu, Ramdin hurried off to get a photographer. Ramdin never let any such opportunity slip by.

Once, when C.H. Atma visited Lucknow, he held a private recital for K.D. Singh Babu in his room in Carlton Hotel. Later, when Ramdin got to know about this, he went to Carlton Hotel and knocked on his door accompanied by a photographer. When C.H. Atma opened the door, Ramdin revealed his identity and purpose of visit. The former had a good laugh and happily obliged Ramdin, thus adding himself to his collection of celebrity photographs. K.D. Singh Babu had a very good rapport with Manna Dey and Ramdin has a very memorable photograph with him too. No celebrity could escape Ramdin and the album has remained his most prized possession.

K.D. Singh Babu himself was a very good classical singer with a mellifluous voice, and when in the right mood, he would recite a K.L. Sehgal number. He was equally at home with old English songs. Once, when we were on a night drive in the Surai range of Pilibhit forest, we made a brief halt for rest in a grassland. K.D. Singh Babu was in a very vibrant mood that day. We had an American guest, one Professor Henry Weaver, also on deputation in Kathmandu at the same time that my father was posted there. K.D. Singh Babu asked all of us if we could sing. As no one came forward, he offered to sing himself. And then we heard him sing a Jim Reeves number, '*O Danny Boy, I love you so*'. He sang beautifully in a high-pitched note and the whole forest reverberated with his voice, enrapturing all of us. It was absolutely amazing. Professor Weaver, who had met him for the first time but knew that he was the Helms Award Winner, said, 'Oh Babu, I thought you were only a top sportsman but now I find that you could have excelled as a good singer too.' Babu truly had the wonderful quality of always being able to enliven a dull moment.

Hockey Babu

Babu is to Indian Hockey what Sir Donald Bradman is to Cricket in Australia.

—Hong Kong Press

Even though he had refused to coach the Indian Olympic team for the 1960 games, owing to differences with the IHF, all his life K.D. Singh remained obsessed with hockey and his singular aim was to see that the younger lot learned the finer points of the game in the same way that he played. He was always in favour of picking up young talented players at school level. The sports school started by him in Lucknow was an example of his dream to produce good players. Speaking to some reporters in Delhi soon after he was nominated as a member of All India Council of Sports, he said, 'Give me twenty-five players from the universities and twenty-five from schools and in three years, you can see the result for yourself.' According to him such a plan would have ensured a continuous flow of good players. He added that there shall be no dearth of good players and the country shall remain on top of the world in hockey. He had always been of the opinion that there was no point in concentrating on senior players who make up the national team, but a nursery like the sports hostel that he started was the right answer.

As reported by *Blitz*, his ability as top-rung organiser was most notably recognised when, after the first defeat of the Indian Olympic Hockey team at the Rome Olympics of 1960, the government of India gave a serious thought to revamping the entire sports scene in the country and the two names that were prominently mentioned were those of Duleepsinhji for cricket and K.D. Singh Babu for hockey.

In 1966, he bagged an assignment to coach a raw, inexperienced Hong Kong team which was slated to participate in the approaching Asian Games to be played in Bangkok. A local newspaper ran a story on him captioned 'Hockey Babu in Hong Kong'. Calling him 'Playboy Prince' because of his regal background, the write-up summarised his character and most notably pointed out that he never liked any interference in his job. It read:

> *Though 42 by the calendar, Babu continues to look lithe and dapper as ever with hardly any signs of the creeping paralysis of age. Breezing in with a big hello and that infectious boyish grin, Babu looked not a day older than that afternoon fifteen years ago when he mounted the victory stand at the Olympic Velodrome in Helsinki to collect a handful of bouquets and a gold medal for India's hockey victory.*
>
> *However, if the years have not taken their toll on this superbly fit athlete, that is only superficial. Due partly to his upbringing and partly to his native genius, Babu is stricken by an inbred snobbishness that is mistaken for superciliousness. But underneath it all, this greatest of all hockey forwards is an extraordinarily likeable and warm-hearted sportsman and is gifted with that rarity among the present crop of sportsmen—the gift of leadership.*
>
> *Tragically enough for Babu, that gift has also been his greatest flaw and undoing. Not only will he not accept fools gladly, but he also makes no bones about telling them where they get off. If, as a skipper of a side, he will stand no direction from anybody on or off the field, the same holds true if he is named coach and asked to take charge of a side.*
>
> *Picture him then in a set-up where not all the officials, talented or otherwise, will stand up for this kind of "prima donna" at the head of a team and you have the answer: Babu, the stick wizard whose artistry and skill nobody dare dispute, managed to play himself out of the Indian hockey team, and sadder still, Indian hockey.*
>
> *If, on that account, one expects to meet a chastened or frustrated young man, the ebullient Babu is anything but that. Effervescent, extroverted and bursting with enthusiasm, Babu has traversed the scene like a human roller-coaster. For a loner, Babu commands the widest range of interests and friends.*
>
> *Not only is he a star hockey player, but he is also a classy batsman in cricket, a better than average tennis player and when he is not doing any of these things, [he] flogs himself to [a] frenzy of excitement as a big game hunter and believe it or not, an angler besides. A brilliant raconteur with a photographic memory, Babu's conversation conjures up in words and pictures a moving*

> *documentary of the sporting scene as he has seen it through almost two decades. The job that Babu has taken on is not an easy one, but the thing that will appeal to him most is that it promises to be challenging. Also, Babu has been given a free hand to mould the players who, by international standards, are mere novices, into a functionally effective team for Bangkok.*
>
> *As to how well he accomplishes it will be of as much interest to Babu as it would be to the Hong Kong Hockey Association which is picking up the tab for his visit here. But if Babu's handiwork is halfway as good as his credentials or build-up, the Indian and Pakistani teams might be in for a few surprises at the Asian Games, Bangkok.*

Soon after coaching was over, Hong Kong's Asian Games squad played an exhibition match against Kowloon Club whom they thrashed by seven goals to nil. But the Indian Olympic player was far from satisfied with the performance of his trainees. 'They are showing off their individual prowess at the expense of team-work,' he snapped at half-time, and then for good measure strode out into the centre of the field barefooted to take personal charge. The improvement was immediate and next day, a local daily highlighted 'Babu shows them how'.

Often, he would call his trainees 'silly gooses' and at the private dinner after the camp was over, they respectfully presented him with a shield on which was inscribed 'To the Master, K.D. Singh Babu from the Silly Gooses Asian Games Trainees 1966'.

Of Babu's work here, the players he trained have been unstinted in their praise.

'I learnt more from Babu than I did playing for Hong Kong at the Tokyo Olympics,' confided Danny Castro. Echoing the same sentiments, another Olympian, Kader Rahman, said, 'This was the first real hockey training I have had in all these years. Babu knows the game. Also, he knows how to correct you whenever you make a mistake.'

He left an indelible impression on many and the press showered accolades on him. One local daily praised him by flashing the headline 'Babu, the Bradman of Indian Hockey'. It further said, 'K.D. Singh Babu is to Indian Hockey what Sir Donald Bradman is to Cricket in Australia.'

Despite the fact that he had called it a day soon after his last appearance at the Nationals in 1958, he remained superbly fit. In 1968, an exhibition match was organised in Delhi between the veteran players of Indian hockey and the Asian Games women's team. The veterans included Major Dhyan Chand, K.D. Singh Babu and Kishen Lal among others. Kishen Lal was the captain of the Indian hockey squad at London Olympics. The Indian veterans defeated the women's team, 3–1, and all the three goals were field goals scored by K.D. Singh Babu. Praising his abilities and fitness, the press flashed a photograph of him in action and wrote, 'Babu defies age. He has shown that he is still as good as he was during the height of his playing career.'

Though India had the honour of retrieving the gold at the 1964 Tokyo Olympics, it failed to repeat a good performance at the 1968 MeElevenco Olympics and had to be satisfied with a bronze. Realising that there was a real need to arrest the decline of Indian hockey, the IHF then again approached K.D. Singh Babu to take charge of the 1972 Munich Olympic-bound team. He accepted the offer but as things turned out, repeated interference by IHF bosses in the selection process greatly affected the performance of the team. Babu had always been of the opinion that Balbir Singh of Railways was the right answer for a fast-moving forward line. Balbir Singh not only showed good stick work but he was also a star athlete with good finishes in 100, 200 and 400 metre track events. His unmatched speed combined with good stick work and powerful finishes was what India needed and it was largely due to him that India thrashed Pakistan at the 1966 Asian Games to get gold. But the IHF bosses outright rejected the idea of his inclusion. He was charged for indiscipline and though Babu tried his level best to convince the federation bosses that he should be given a free hand in the selection of the team, continued interference is what harmed India.

Another point of conflict was the selection of the goalkeeper. In his opinion, a fast-moving forward line and a good custodian were the back bone of any team but the IHF bosses refused to relent. India topped its pool, but in the semi-final against Pakistan, the absence of a good finisher in the striking circle like Balbir Singh let a lot of chances go a begging and then again it was the Indian custodian who let India down by bad anticipation. Interference by IHF bosses had again shown what harm it had done to Indian hockey right from 1956 and India had to be satisfied with a bronze again. Here, one needs to go back to the warning cries of the celebrated sports critic A.F.S. (Bobby) Talyarkhan about the decline of Indian hockey standards due to the interference by the new IHF set-up which had begun in the 50s soon after Naval Tata relinquished the post of IHF President. Save for the 1964 Tokyo Olympics and the Asian Games of 1966, India hardly had any reasons to cheer. And then finally at the 1976 Montreal Olympics, India was ignominiously pushed down to seventh position.

The Final Whistle

Long Live Babu, you have done wonders.

—Standing ovation by over 40,000 spectators when his school trainees defeated a star-studded Indian Airlines team in 1977

As mentioned in the previous chapter, K.D. Singh Babu always nursed the idea that in any sport, it is always advisable to concentrate on the young. According to him, it was easier to convert straw into gold as compared to those players who already had a fixed idea of their own and could not be reformed. This is exactly why he started a sports hostel in Lucknow and took personal chargc to teach hockey in typical textbook fashion. He was the first person to bring hockey on to the blackboard. According to him, hockey was not just about hit-and-run; rather, it had to be played with brains. Commenting about his superlative mastermind, former Olympian Aslam Sher Khan is on record as having said, 'He was the only person who demonstrated on the field what he told on the board.' Even during the time when he was a participating member of any team, he was always consulted by fellow players to give them useful tips. That this was true became clear when in 1960, he was requested by the IHF to coach the Rome-bound team after he refused to be a part of the team even though he had been selected.

Though the debacle at Munich Olympics came as a great shock to him, he was determined to go ahead with his plans for revival of hockey in the country. He was like a winner who never quit and continued to concentrate on the youngsters of the Lucknow sports hostel. As time passed, the youngsters of his nursery started to bloom. Thirteen of his trainees made a national mark and some were even selected for the Olympic side. Not only that, what I believe is that the cream of the lot even managed to land jobs on this foundation. His cherished desire was not only to see emergence of good international players from all segments of sports but also to always be there to lend a helping hand to get them jobs.

By mid 1977, he started showing signs of illness which was diagnosed as mild depression, and yet any matter about hockey used to bring him back into his old elements. To promote hockey, he used to organise an All India Hockey Tournament in Lucknow which became an annual affair. Selected top teams of the country were invited to participate in this tournament and players got a chance to showcase their talent. Though it was never a platform for selection for the national side, it always had a noticeable effect.

In the All India Tournament of 1977, which was held sometime in the month of November, the finals were made by Indian Airlines and Lucknow Eleven. The star-studded Indian Airlines team was led by Olympian Inam-ur-Rehman. Apart from other top players of the country, this team also had Major Dhyan Chand's son, Ashok Kumar, who took part in the 1972 Munich Olympics. The Lucknow Eleven players were youngsters from the sports hostel. Incidentally, while K.D. Singh Babu was the official coach for Indian Airlines at that time, the Lucknow Eleven youngsters were his juvenile trainees. Also playing for Lucknow Eleven was Syed Ali who had represented India at the 1976 Montreal Olympics, but he too was a product of this hostel. The scenario was set for a dramatic clash between these two teams, both of which were under Babu's training.

A mammoth crowd of more than 40,000 had gathered to watch this great event. The atmosphere was charged and electrifying. Seated by the sideline was the great maestro, K.D. Singh Babu himself. His teams were facing each other and the battle lines were drawn. A Mahabharata was about to begin, but with a difference. This Dronacharya was only passively involved. As he was the official coach of the Airlines team, he was seen giving useful tips to the Airlines players before commencement of the match. By half-time, no one of the teams could score. Jasvinder Singh, who was playing for Lucknow Eleven as a right-half, recalls:

> *K.D. Singh Babu then came to our camp before the start of the second half and discussed a certain strategy. He had obviously detected a chink in the armour of the Airlines defense and told us to exploit that. We did as he advised. And soon as per the plan given to us by him, Syed Ali gave a cross to Rakesh Srivastava who did not miss and Lucknow Eleven scored the only goal of the match. We won by 1–0.*

The moment the final whistle was blown, the entire crowd stood up in a thunderous applause, shouting in a unified voice: 'Babu Zindabad, tumne kamal kar diya!' (Long live Babu, you have done wonders!) That day, though unwell, K.D. Singh Babu had a smile on his face and he glowed with radiance once again. After the match was over and as told to me by Jasvinder Singh, some disheartened Airlines players walked up to Babu and asked him as to what tips he had given to the Lucknow Eleven boys. Babu just smiled and looked towards the crowd who were still shouting 'Zindabad' as the whole of the stadium was reverberating with joyous excitement.

It was not Lucknow Eleven that had won but it was K.D. Singh Babu who had won the hearts of thousands. He had shown what a master strategist he was. He mingled with the crowd and almost everyone wanted to shake hands with him. Walking like a colossus through a maze of human waves that were surging towards him to shake hands, he had sent a message to the corridors of hockey officials. A message, loud and clear, that had they heeded his advice years ago, India would never have lost her glory. As fate beheld, this was the last show of this greatest-of-the-great sportsmen of the country. He had proven his point by showing them how.

By the beginning of March 1978, his health deteriorated further but no one knew what problem was afflicting him. One day, while he was coming out of his office, a teenage school girl approached him for an autograph. He looked down at her and obliged her with a note, 'Give a smile to one who has no one'. Obviously his note was a reflection of his own problem. That boyish infectious smile had vanished and he was finding it hard to get it back. As the month of March drew to a close, he totally stopped attending office. In the wee hours of 28 March, he left his bedroom quietly and moved to an unoccupied room of his rented accommodation where he shot himself with his gun. A gun that had nearly ended his playing career about thirty-two years back returned to take his life. He left this world with a bang, shocking millions of fans. A bang similar to the one the world had heard when he announced his arrival in the year 1937 during the Trades Cup in Delhi at the tender age of sixteen by flooring Olympic players. 'Hockey Babu', the Bradman of Indian hockey, had finally bid adieu to the world.

As family and friends gathered, we found a book by the side of his pillow. He had been reading it the night before. It was *My Sunny Days* by

Sunil Gavaskar. One great had been reading about another great. At no time could he keep himself away from sports.

While his mortal remains lay on the floor, we saw a young Sikh gentleman sitting by the side of his body, holding on to his feet. He was weeping bitterly. I approached this young man and asked, 'Who are you, no one of us have seen you before?' With tears flowing down his face, he turned towards me and narrated his story:

> *One day, I was being taken to Hazratgunj police station by two constables when Babu sahib happened to pass by in his car. By the grace of God, he happened to look towards us and then all of a sudden, he stopped. He then asked the two constables about the problem and as they replied that I was wanted by the inspector, he asked the three of us to get into the back of the car and drove off to the police station. There he talked to the inspector and got me released. I had really done nothing for which I was being harassed. After the ordeal was over, he brought me back to his office and comforted me. After some time, when he felt that now I was out of shock, he asked me if I participated in any sporting event. By that time, some of his subordinate staff had also gathered there. When I said no, I do not play any games, he laughed and gesturing at some, said, "Look, this young man has such a good physique and he does not play. What a pity." Then he turned towards me and said, "Look young man, I am quite sure that you can be a good sportsman and I can see that you can be a good track athlete, that is if you try out." Without waiting for an answer from me, he ordered someone to get a pair of spikes of my size. The very next moment, we were all in the field and I was made to run several times. My speed was being clocked and after the initial test was over, he told me, "Look, you have done well and now with a bit of regular training you will do excellently." Thereafter, I became a regular and with the passing of time, he got me a job. Whatever I am today, it is just because of him. That fateful day, when the policemen were taking me in handcuffs, he descended like an angel and saved me from an ignominious and dreadful life.*

As I come to the end of writing this book, I wonder if this particular Sikh gentleman would ever re-surface with a copy of this biography.

A hockey stick was placed on his funeral pyre and the next day, a local daily carried a photograph of the same. Underneath it was written: 'United in death, they score the ultimate goal'. In an obituary, *Sports and Pastime* said everything in just three words: 'A Rare Genius'.

This biography is my humble tribute to him. Kunwar Digvijay Singh 'Babu' lived true to his name: 'The World Conqueror'. Not only did he rule in the field, he also lives on in the hearts of all those whom he helped.

About the Author

Born in 1946 at Barabanki, Raghavendra Singh did his formal schooling in Colvin Taluqdar's College in Lucknow. He completed his post-graduate studies in Botany from Lucknow University and joined the Department of Botany, Bareilly College in 1968. Later on, he switched his major subject and completed post-graduate studies in Zoology from Agra University. He also served as Lecturer in the Department of Zoology, Bareilly College, Bareilly, till 1972.

He is a well-known mango orchardist of the state and pioneered the technique of mango pruning for increased production, a method that has not only become a subject of discussion in mango circles but has also been widely accepted and recognised as a result of widespread newspaper coverage.

In 1979, he went to the UK to work on pheasants, and received a diploma from the World Pheasant Association for excellent work. He and his father (Late) Dr Kr Suresh Singh were the first to breed endangered Cheer pheasant under tropical conditions in Lucknow for re-introduction in the Kumaon Himalayas.

Raghavendra Singh has co-authored (with his father) three publications on the subject of pheasants. The first, Pheasants, Birds Par Excellence, was published by WWF in 1982 and released at the 2nd International Symposium at Srinagar, Kashmir. This was followed by two other publications, *pheasants of India*, a small illustrated booklet about the various species found in India and *Pheasants of India, and their Aviculture* (1995) which were published by Wildlife Institute of India, Dehradun.

He is a keen golfer and in his early years, has played for the Hockey Eleven of his school as also cricket at club level.

Raghavendra Singh currently lives on the outskirts of Lucknow, taking keen interest in gardening and bird watching. For several years, he has maintained avid interest in wildlife in general and many of his articles were published by the Lucknow edition of a leading English daily as opinion columns. In 1991, he was nominated to the UP State Wildlife Advisory Board.